MW00658247

GOOD

BETTER

BEST!

Fostering Good Work Habits in Children

Scepter

Published by Scepter Publishers, P.O. Box 1391, New Rochelle, NY 10802
www.scepterpublishers.org

Printed in the United States of America

ISBN: 978-1-59417-191-8

GOOD

BETTER

BEST!

Fostering Good Work Habits in Children

Esther Joos Esteban, Ph.D.

Dedicated to Mama and Papa who facilitated opportunities and training in work-related virtues

CONTENTS

CHAPTER 1 Good, Better, Best: *Diligence in Work*

CHAPTER 2 Laundry Day: *Order in Work*

CHAPTER 3 A Working Mama:
Responsibility in Work

CHAPTER 4 A Summer Block Party:
Cooperation in Work

CHAPTER 5 **Pancake Day:**
Cheerfulness in Work

ACKNOWLEDGMENTS

To those who answered my call to participate in writing this book, a heartfelt thank you for your support and insights. I wanted to analyze the process of working and investigate the practice of work-related virtues that empower children to attain excellence in their work. My quest required the input of many: family, friends, colleagues, students, parents, caregivers, teachers, and seminar participants. Special appreciation extends to:

- **Family:** husband Enrique; daughters and sons-in-law Christine and Ajay Munshi and Cynthia and Andreas Coppi; sons Enrique and Jose Antonio; grandchildren—Nikhil, Mayuri, Carlo, and Marco; sister Loretta Saunderson, who shared her memories and reaffirmed our childhood experiences; and niece Pamela Voelksen.

- **Interviewees:** Trixie Abadilla, Diane van Ausdall, Sara Brescher, Angela Camacho, Socorro Claudio, Anna Gomez de Liano, Judy Henderson, Gail Lewis, Linda Mabanta, Inge Mills, Tessie Moran, Carol Morris, Dr. Gerard O'Malley, Carol Pilone, Patricia Posner, Gail Russakov, Leticia Sala, Nancy Sieffert, Carol Tan, Lianne Tiu, Rita Tuason, Tootsie Vicente, Carla Villacorta, Raffaela Yurecko.

- **Professional Educators:** Colleagues at the University of Asia & the Pacific-School of Education, Manila: Dean Celerino Tiongo, Dr. Angel Antonio, Dr. Riza Bondal, Concha de la Cruz, Dr. Joyce Dy, Lexie Estacio, Dr. Gladys Golo, Dr. Ernesto Grio, Carl Moog, Dr. Ferdinand Pingul, and Gizelle Tan. Other educators: Stella Alcantara and the Maria Montessori Foundation, Manila; Carlo Carino and the teachers of the Maria Montessori Children's School, Manila; Dr. Thomas Lickona; Dr. James Stenson; and my students in the courses I teach at the University of Asia & the Pacific: Developmental Psychology, Instructional Leadership and Supervision, Lifespan Development, and Media Literacy for Educators.

- **Survey Respondents:** Lita Alegre, Eden Binaday, Lysette Caruz, Marguerite Franceski, Marilou Gatchalan, Victoria Huang, Virginia Jadro, Nina Lagdameo, Marietta De Lucia, Jill Kierulf, Antonella Lazar, Huo Qian Ru, Amanda del Rosario, Edna and Peter Tanchuling, and all those respondents who submitted the survey anonymously.

- **Friends, many of whom are teachers:** Cynthia Ballat, Jimeno Damaso, Nanette Diyco, Rhoda Lubetkin, Lydia Olano, Soldead Navarro, Lourdes Romero.
- **Scepter Publishers:** publishers John Powers and Nathan Davis; editor Russell Shaw; and proofreader Arlene Borg.
- **St. Josemaría Escrivá** for his inspiration and exemplary practice of work-related virtues.

INTRODUCTION

In 1946 Mama acquired her first Singer sewing machine. The monotonous sound generated by her steady foot-pedaling signaled that she was busy sewing us new dresses or mending old clothes. Each year on Easter Sunday our neighbors gathered outside our home to see what we sisters would be wearing. They marveled at our outfits, even spring coats and hats, sewn by the hands of Mrs. Joos.

Long before housewives in our neighborhood owned clothes dryers, they hung out their laundry to dry under the sun. Mama noted a need for a handy way to carry the wooden clothespins that would hold the towels and clothing in place. To facilitate the process, she designed and sewed beautiful apron-like clothespin bags to be worn when hanging out the wash. She chose two colorful complementary pieces of cloth and rickrack for décor. By creating an inner pouch for handy storage of the clothespins, her practical design helped accomplish the work.

Friends, neighbors, and teachers at school felt honored and grateful to receive Mama's clothespin bags; this became her trademark gift on birthdays and holidays. What started out as a useful solution to a domestic task evolved into a hobby that was an outlet for her creativity and remarkable self-giving.

Whereas Papa's black metal lunch box symbolized his work ethic, Mama's sewing machine came to represent her dedication to full-time homemaking. When she eventually returned to a career in sales, Mama decided it was time to trade in her old sewing machine for a more efficient electrical model. She did so reluctantly and felt like she was losing an old trusted friend.

. . . .

Mothers and fathers are the original human resource managers. Whatever the era or circumstances, their challenges remain constant: to pass on a legacy of positive work attitudes and to foster work-related habits. Mama and Papa were a good team. They laid the groundwork that we children, grandchildren, and now great-grandchildren struggle hard to imitate.

A funny thing happened on the way to writing this sequel to *The Work of Children*. I realized with hindsight that in our family Papa essentially articulated the *meaning*, *purpose*, and *value* of work. Through his homespun wisdom and rules, he made work a natural, ordinary, and extraordinary activity that filled our lives. But it was really our beloved Mama who translated Papa's theories into practice.

In *Good, Better, Best,* Mama's role is examined. By recalling examples of how she provided a role model for work-related virtues, I illustrate her crucial task of training and development. Her quiet, unassuming contributions are highlighted in the introductions to the chapters that follow.

Good, Better, Best takes the exploration of children's work a step beyond its predecessor. Understanding work is a prerequisite, but application is its natural follow-up. A nine year old may know she has to do her homework, but how well does she complete the assignment? A five year old may understand that he has to straighten up his toys, but how does he approach his task? An adolescent on the school football team may memorize the plays, but how conscientious is he about going to practice? A teenager may be very sensitive to belonging in a group, but how good a team player is he? A preteen may follow a homework routine faithfully, but does she go about her studies with gloom and dread? To assure completion of their tasks, children need to develop work-related virtues.

In this volume, five specific work-related virtues or good habits are emphasized***: diligence, order, responsibility, cooperation,*** and ***cheerfulness***. They are the building blocks of good work. Rather than random or occasional attempts to get something done, they are purposeful and sustained approaches that take time and considerable training to develop.

The Work of Children identified work as "a dynamic universal process; any decent worthwhile human activity; a channel to develop individual capabilities and talents; a means to human perfection and sanctity; a means to transform someone or something; and an opportunity to help and be of service."[1]

More specifically, work translates into a ***task,*** an ***activity, process, duty, challenge,*** or an ***opportunity*** that finds its outlets in ***play, study, chores, hobbies, sports, and other extracurricular activities***. As primary educators, parents explain, give examples, demonstrate, tell stories, and role model good work. They may use a wide range of strategies to help children find meaning, purpose, and value in work. That's the easy part! Getting children to *do* the work voluntarily and *sustain* and *complete* tasks are the hard parts. These are the challenges that *Good, Better, Best* confronts.

Encouraged by the positive feedback from readers of *The Work of Children*, the same format is followed. Every chapter begins with a personal memory to introduce a theme, i.e., one of the five virtues. *Fast Forward* relates the challenges and issues to present-day realities. Suggested techniques that facilitate habit formation at successive stages of development follow in *Opportune Moments.* Integrated into the discussions of each stage is a selected *Problem in the Process* examining a likely hindrance. At the end of every chapter, *Quotables* present wise insights about work and invite the reader to add personal thoughts.

This second volume aims to be another guide, reference, or manual for parents, caregivers, and educators. Names in anecdotes have been fictionalized except when permission was given to use someone's real name.

Esther Joos Esteban
New York City, 2013

CHAPTER 1

GOOD, BETTER, BEST: *Diligence in Work*

Report Card Day

While some of us giggled nervously and a few trembled, we waited for the distribution of report cards. It was the day of reckoning at Mount Vernon Avenue Public Elementary School; we third graders took it pretty seriously. Papa and Mama knew exactly what day to expect our progress reports. My sister, Loretta, and I were good students and did them proud over the years by earning mostly As and Bs.

The scene played like an old broken record when we returned home to show our cards. Mama and Papa looked at our grades, then looked at each other, then looked at us, and said:

Good, better, best,
Never let me rest
Until my good is better
And my better best.

Loretta and I had grown accustomed to the routine and the predictable reactions of our Mama and Papa.

Finally, one grading period, I surprised even myself and got all As.

"Wow!" I thought. "I wonder what Mama and Papa will say this time? Better yet, I wonder what they will give me—maybe some chocolates or a new doll. Maybe they will forget to say that silly poem!"

With high anticipation, I showed the card to them and watched their faces carefully for an indication of something to come! It came all right.

Beaming with pride, Mama looked at Papa who was also beaming, and once again said,

Good, better, best,
Never let me rest
Until my good is better
And my better best.

Disappointed? Well, maybe I was a little. But I knew it was their way of sending important messages: *Good work! Keep it up! There is always room for improvement.*

Mama and Papa never showed anger or disappointment; neither did they ridicule our efforts. Throughout our schooling, they applauded us in triumphs and encouraged us during setbacks. What they valued most was our *diligence* to finish a task and struggles to try our best. They were our first mentors in a lifetime journey that would aim for excellence in work.

....

'Good, better, best' was meant to motivate and inspire us to keep trying, not to pressure us with unreasonable expectations. No doubt, Mama and Papa set high standards for us children, but they did not impose the unrealistic demands of obsessive-compulsive work addicts. Yes, Mama wrote her daily lists of 'things to do,' but these were essentially reminders. If the list was not completed, she simply carried the tasks over to the next day. And when Papa undertook a task (whether inventing a tool or building a crib for my doll), he did so with joy, precision, and punctuality. He set reasonable time frames to finish tasks.

Mama and Papa did not suffer from the anxiety of perfectionists whose work is never good enough. They helped us appreciate that oftentimes the best is the enemy of the good. It is more important to be prudent and realistic about what can be accomplished, without adhering to a rigid time schedule or agonizing over whether the outcome is perfect.

These memories of Mama and Papa (the latter in *The Work of Children*) show how two hard-working parents gave lessons in work and set the example that started us on our journey toward the pursuit of excellence.

Diligence Defined

Diligence is persevering effort. It is characterized by steady, earnest, and persistent application. Without diligence, a task will likely be executed halfheartedly or reluctantly; it may have a mediocre or unfinished product.

Training in the habit of diligence guides children to develop their capacity to pay attention to the requirements of a task, produce quality work, bear difficulties, and endure obstacles calmly and without complaint.

Diligence is not practiced in isolation. Other key habits that are most directly related to the exercise of *diligence* are:

- Patience or uncomplaining endurance
- Cheerfulness or joy of spirit and optimism
- Temperance or self-control and self-regulation
- Fortitude or courageous perseverance
- Prudence or sound judgment and conscience
- Responsibility or accountability for thoughts, words, actions

These related habits recur throughout our discussions.

Virtues Revisited

At a time when the development of virtues sounded like a quaint, old-fashioned quest, several books surfaced, e.g., *The Seven Habits of Highly Effective People* (Covey 1989), *The Book of Virtues* (Bennett 1993), *Twenty Teachable Virtues* (Unell and Wyckoff 1995), *Seven Habits of Highly Effective Teens* (Covey 1998), *Compass* (Stenson 2003) *Character Matters* (Lickona 2004). These books have generated a renewed appreciation of the profound importance of virtues.

Thomas Lickona, author of books on character education, views work-related virtues as crucial to character building. He identifies *diligence* and *order* as virtues needed for best work, whereas *cooperation, responsibility*, and *cheerfulness* strengthen best relationships.

Even at a young age children have the potential to decide and act. This capacity empowers them to make decisions freely and independently; act on decisions; take consequences; exercise self-discipline; sustain actions; persevere; make moral choices; and practice virtues.

Virtues are *good habits* that seek truth and goodness as their goals. Virtues are acquired through continuous and intense training, conscious effort, and repetition until the habits are performed easily, quickly, constantly, readily, and naturally. When parents and caregivers exert effort toward habit formation, they participate in one of the noblest goals of education: to lead children in a life of virtue. The opposite of virtues are vices. Vices are likewise habits, but they are detours from truth and goodness and may develop into nasty, out-of-control addictions.

While Mama and Papa were sensitive to obstacles in the development of diligence, they had a firm grasp of childrearing. In the 1950s, they fretted occasionally about what might challenge their efforts to develop diligence. They were especially concerned about the availability of too many toys on the market or the possibility of addiction to television!

They did not waver, however, in asserting their parental authority. They articulated and upheld clear moral values, set limitations on behavior, and without hesitation applied sanctions when we misbehaved. If we had homework assignments, we finished them before dinner; if we were assigned a school project, we were expected to complete what we started. If we were assigned a household chore, we did it before play. When we practiced the violin and piano, we stopped only after the agreed-upon practice time. If we wanted a new toy, we waited until our birthday. In the process, Mama and Papa honed the development of virtues. We sisters perceived these practices as natural and good.

Mama and Papa balanced expectations and restrictions with affection and encouragement. Childrearing sixty years ago was a matter of basic necessities and simple strategies. During the postwar years of middle-income America, we children observed parents who fostered economic recovery, worked hard, and upheld family solidarity.

Fast Forward

Parents and children in the new millennium deal with more complex issues: breakdown of the family and parental authority; anti-values; excessive materialism; emphasis on lifestyles, and the enormous impact of media. Surrounded by malls that project blatant consumerism and engulfed by a multimedia environment, parents, caregivers, and teachers confront situations and dilemmas that require decisiveness and resolution.

A New York City child psychologist relates the question that a preteen client asked when he arrived for his first consultation: "Is it okay if I play a computer game while we talk?" When the therapist responded with a firm "no," the child was shocked by her decisive, no-nonsense answer. Apparently he was not used to having his parents decline his requests or demands. To his credit, he accepted her authority respectfully.

Overwhelmed by the demands of parenting in the new millennium and bombarded by the advice of a multitude of experts, parenting nowadays is necessarily transformed into a businesslike 'management by objectives.'

"What kind of a child do we want to raise?"

"How will we do it?"

Whatever the family constellation, parents need to do some periodic reevaluation in order to fulfill the purposeful and extraordinary calling of parenting. For a parent who is raising a child on his or her own or for blended families, the questions are the same, although solutions are more intricate. Periodically parents may need some retooling or fine tuning of skills in order to hone the virtue of diligence. This is what worked for some parents.

The Home Setting

Already as young parents with a clear agenda in mind, Rae and Bill raised their three children by mutual agreement. They devised techniques to help the children internalize self-discipline and sustain efforts. Starting in toddlerhood and continuing into early childhood, they nipped tantrums in the bud. By being distracted to another activity, or through a simple 'no' or shake of the head, the children slowly got the message when their behavior was not appropriate or unacceptable. By being read stories such as *The Little Engine that Could*, the children learned that with self-control and perseverance almost anything is possible. Through a slow process that entailed much patience, repetition, and lots of affection, their children responded positively. As the children matured, Rae and Bill used dialogue and explanations to foster diligence. Rather than shouts, put-downs, or 'reverse psychology,' they respected the dignity of each child. No-nonsense, straightforward questions and requests were especially effective with their adolescents. Because Rae and Bill were sensitive to developing maturity in their children, their teenagers rose to the occasion and tried harder to measure up to their parents' reasonable expectations.

Characterized by her nonstop energy, solo working parent Inge is a model of endurance and perseverance. Her enthusiasm is contagious and her explanations to her three children have taken root. "Once you start something, you make a commitment and must complete the task. Don't give up, even when you meet hardships. Work with what you have and know that I am here for you." Her steadfast support has inspired them to finish what they undertake.

Ajay shared his experiences of how he developed an interest in sports and diligence in his nine-year-old son, Nikhil. He started in the earliest years by rolling a ball to his toddler son. When he noticed that Nik was able to catch a ball, Ajay moved things up a notch. They spent fun time together playing catch in nearby parks. In time, Ajay started to expose Nik to a wide array of sports, e.g., soccer, basketball, flag football, swimming. In the process, he gradually identified his son's preferences and aptitudes. While Ajay encouraged understanding and self-confidence, Nik narrowed his choice of sports, developing his defensive skills in flag football. In his first season, he just couldn't manage to pull a flag, but he kept working at it until he became one of the coaches' "go-to" players on defense. Originally, Nik disliked playing defense because he wanted to catch passes and score touchdowns, but he came to embrace it and now actually looks forward to the role of being the "defensive stopper" on his team. He even bought a set of his own flags at a sporting goods store so that Ajay could wear them and he could practice pulling them.

Father and son started rooting for their favorite football team and now share in the excitement of play-offs. Ajay buys sports books for birthdays, and father and son play their favorite Wii sports video games to reinforce an understanding of games and team play. Nik has learned a lot about perseverance, self-improvement, and the importance of everyone fulfilling his designated role on a team.

Unless he is sick, Nik never misses practices. He draws satisfaction and joy from his increasing skills and team contributions. He is developing diligence through steady, earnest attention, and energetic application. Father and son have bonded through their mutual interest.

Parenting a military family with frequent moves and adjustments required clear-cut strategies. Judy and Russ explained to their three children that no matter where they were assigned, every family member continued to play an important role for coherent, integrated family life. "Daddy's work is in the military, mine is in the home, and yours is in school. We each have a job to do, we try our best, and we finish our work no matter where we are," explained Judy.

Parents Rae, Bill, Inge, Ajay, Judy, and Russ approached diligence training by using techniques that demanded thought, action, and persistence interspersed with just the right amounts of encouragement and praise. Beyond all of their conscious efforts, however, was their noteworthy and inspiring role-modeling.

The School Setting

My sister Loretta, an experienced teacher in public middle school, welcomed yet another six-week cycle of students to her German language class. She had been forewarned about several students who were known to be disruptive. As predicted, they sat at the back of the classroom on the first day of class and started to act up. Loretta proceeded to explain the contents and objectives of the course and declared unexpected classroom policies.

"We are about to begin an exciting journey into another land and language. In my class, I allow my students to choose their own seats. In two days' time, please sit in the seat where you will do your *best work*. Furthermore, no one fails in this class."

She got their immediate attention. Thinking that the course would be a pushover, the students started to buzz among themselves. Loretta explained further.

"There is no need for failure if everyone does his or her best work. I shall judge your work in *my* class on your best efforts basis! You have a chance to start anew. In the next six weeks, I shall give you ten opportunities to prove yourself in assignments, projects, and quizzes."

Through another policy, she encouraged them to choose a typical German name which they were to use as their own during the coming six weeks. This practice always met with enthusiasm by her students. Not only did they familiarize themselves with German names, but it was a subtle, clever way of giving them all, including the potential troublemakers, a clean slate.

By the third day, everyone had chosen a seat. The so-called troublemakers all sat in the front of the classroom and performed optimally during the grading period. With her firm but friendly control, the students sensed a teacher who was sincere, concerned, and respectful of their dignity. She set high expectations, encouraged individual abilities, and developed self-worth. She was consistent in her implementation of classroom rules and policies, and they knew she meant business; she earned their respect and trust. She was unwavering in her encouragement of perseverance and diligence.

Daily in a multicultural setting that included at least fifteen nationalities in any given class, Loretta was fondly called *the Frau*. Her students knew she was giving them every possible opportunity to develop excellence in their work of the moment: study!

In keeping with a family tradition of educators, niece Pamela V. is a middle school science teacher. Conscientious, well organized, friendly, quick-witted, and no-nonsense, Mrs. V. gets results. Reggie, one of her pupils, was frequently called to the Guidance Department because of misconduct in other classes. He was asked by the counselor, "Why are you doing so well in Mrs. V.'s science class?"

Reggie responded quickly: "Her subject is so interesting. She works hard. We really want to try our best." Two generations removed, Mama and Papa's legacy of 'good, better, best' found root in a granddaughter who upheld their positive attitudes and habits.

The struggle for diligence and excellence, however, may sometimes backfire in the school setting. Gifted programs or advance placement courses that aim at honing the special abilities of selected students may give students a false sense of superiority. They may develop an "I'm better than you" attitude, which could undermine socialization with students in other courses. Also when students who are continually extolled as the best face competition or setbacks, they may not be able to cope with the implications and realities of failure.

Sometimes, achievement of the best becomes an obstacle to attainment of the good. When team coaches, parents, or alumni become fixated only on winning and exert excessive, unreasonable pressure on team members, the players may lose out on the more important lessons of sportsmanship, team spirit, grace under pressure, and coping with defeat.

When parents live vicariously through their child's achievements and prioritize their own hidden agenda of personal prestige, they send wrong signals about the goals of work. "Parents are preoccupied with 'a narrow and shortsighted vision of success' that expects children 'to provide status and meaning in their lives.' It's a harmful combination, weighing kids down with serious issues—stress, exhaustion, depression, anxiety, poor coping skills, and unhealthy reliance on others for support and direction, and a weak sense of self."[1]

Early Childhood: *Small Beginnings*

The foundations for the exercise of diligence are laid in the first six years of life. Experiences can range from joyful exuberance to early frustration.

If she thinks there is an opportunity to participate or help, six-year-old Maya runs to get her footstool so that she can reach the countertop where Christine is baking. "What do you want me to do, Mommy? What can I do to help?" Her willingness reflects a natural inner need and eagerness of young children to learn and do. Mom wisely plans ahead exactly what she wants to teach her daughter, i.e., those skills within the child's capabilities. Maya already knows how to carefully spoon dough into cupcake tins, spread frosting on the cooled cupcakes, and decorate cupcakes with colorful sprinkles. Today she will learn a new skill: packaging the cupcakes to give as take-home gifts.

Maya understands that if she starts to bake with Mommy, she has to finish her tasks. All twenty-four cupcakes must be ready for the family get-together. Beyond the challenge of her work, however, the youngster wants to make the family happy with freshly baked goodies. Best of all, Maya loves to spend time with Mommy.

Four-year-old Carlo has a special talent for drawing. Lately he has been sketching his favorite superheroes with remarkable details as shown in their masks and capes. When the results don't look just right, Carlo gets frustrated and impatient with himself. Mom Cindy and dad Andreas explain, "Sometimes we have to live with mistakes and our work may not always be perfect. It's important to try again." Cindy sits a while with Carlo as he discovers a new technique and repeats his sketches. This time, Carlo is satisfied with his work.

Through the patient training of his parents Pamela and John, Connor, age five, has developed a night-time habit of cleaning up his toys before going to bed. When Grandma offers to help, he explains that there is a bin or shelf for every item. If Grandma doesn't get his instructions quite right, Connor doesn't hesitate to correct her and demonstrate the right way! Connor knows that tidying up is not a hit-or-miss task; he is preparing his room for another day of play.

At this stage of development, young children are basically willing to help and eager to please parents, caregivers, and teachers.

Opportune Moments

Although virtue-building is a dynamic process that starts in the earliest years and continues for a lifetime, this book focuses only on early childhood, middle childhood, and adolescence. To put theory into practice, *Opportune Moments* offer practical approaches in the art and craft of forming children in virtues. Essentially, these teachable moments aim to: provoke thought about work; establish objectives of a task; suggest strategies for implementation; encourage perseverance; and reassess efforts. Among all the suggestions, role modeling is the constant variable.

The struggle to put good habits into practice is a cumulative process. Crucial foundations are laid in early childhood; this can be seen by the numerous suggestions of survey respondents. If training and opportunities in the first stage are lacking or weak, then the habits ought to be developed and strengthened in the next stage until they evolve into virtues or stable qualities of the human personality. If virtue formation is neglected, the struggle in adolescence is formidable and the potential to develop the opposite bad habits, or vices, increases. The struggle, however, continues and can succeed.

In *Opportune Moments,* stories and practical recommendations suggested by parents illustrate the dynamics of the process.

Opportune Moments

To foster diligence in Early Childhood (3–6 years)

- Begin with 'little things' or small steps and gradually lead up to more complex tasks.

- If possible, prepare a sample of what is expected or demonstrate how to do the task.
- When a child first begins a task, try to facilitate small experiences of 'success' in overcoming difficulties. This will encourage him/her to try again.
- Show delight in the child's efforts and energy to do an activity or task well.
- Praise the child when he/she repeats good efforts.
- Use simple extrinsic motivators, e.g., encouragement or occasional prizes (like simple stickers), to facilitate the development of a habit.
- When the task has become a habit, discontinue or lessen extrinsic rewards lest the child rely heavily on external motivation.
- When the child finishes playing with a toy, suggest that he/she choose a progressively more difficult one, e.g., a jigsaw puzzle.
- Encourage the child to explore, try new toys, activities, or tasks to build confidence in him/herself.
- If the child frets, complains, or wants to give up, give some assistance and foster patience and optimism. Then recognize, "I can see you tried really hard" or "I like the way you colored the picture. It looks good." It is best to praise the work and encourage the worker; this encourages resilience and perseverance.
- Display the child's drawings, paintings, constructions, and sculptures to show appreciation for his or her creativity and efforts.
- Maintain a sense of humor. Try to keep things lighthearted.
- If the task or activity is truly beyond the child's capabilities, then reset expectations and try another approach or task within his/her capacity.
- Repeat instructions, as necessary, until the child is able to begin an activity or task on his/her own. In this way he/she develops independence and a sense of accomplishment.
- Encourage the child to self-check his/her own work and then show or explain it to an adult.

- In a relaxed and natural manner without rigidity or punishments, patiently remind the child to do a chore. Give a helping hand, if necessary, but don't do the task for him/her.
- Be consistent in the implementation of tasks. A haphazard approach may confuse the child or discourage momentum.
- If the child does sloppy or incomplete work in an unacceptable manner, give one-on-one assistance, if necessary. Require the child to repeat the task.
- Thank the child for his/her help and efforts. This builds self-confidence and shows good manners.
- Gradually explain and remind the child of the positive consequences of persevering and trying one's best. Young children find joy and satisfaction in doing things well.
- Give the child an early start in the habit of diligence. The child is learning to set standards for him/herself that lead to excellence in work.
- ROLE MODEL DILIGENCE.

A Problem in the Process: Lack of Self-Regulation

During the early years, children are in the process of gaining emotional control and self-regulation. Parents, caregivers, and teachers can expect temper tantrums and 'melt-downs.' Not only do young children need to understand what they are doing, how they feel, and why it may be wrong or unsafe, they need gradually to develop self-regulation or "control of behavior to conform to a caregiver's demands or expectation, even when the caregiver is not present."[2]

Because foundations for diligence are laid during the first six years, problems need early detection and remediation. Children need systematic training to get in the habit of gaining emotional control. The following scenario presents a situation that could undermine the early stage of training in self-regulation and diligence.

Paul and Susanne are working parents who spend many hours away from home managing their own business. They entrust the care of their youngest child Terrie, age 3, to a nanny, Sue, who spoils and overprotects the child. Sue does not allow Terrie to feed or dress herself, or help clean up her toys. The child eats snacks or watches TV any time she wants. No limits are set on Terrie's tantrums. Overcompensating for their absences, Paul and Susanne spoil their young daughter with new toys.

Self-indulged and without training in acceptable standards of behavior, Terrie is on a disaster path that will hinder emotional control and self-regulation. With no:

- expectations and limitations set,
- explanations and instructions given,
- training in how to gain emotional control,
- consistency in the implementation of controls,
- choices given to foster simple decision-making,
- encouragement to keep trying, and
- experience or satisfaction in persevering in a task,

how will Terrie develop diligence?

Parents Paul and Susanne are hard-working and persevering role models; unfortunately, Terrie never sees them in action. She does not witness their good example. Children are great imitators; they need to catch their parents and caregivers in the act of self-regulation and exercise of diligence.

The crucial importance of developing emotional control and self-regulation are reinforced by the theory of Emotional Intelligence or EI. It is an ability or skill in perceiving, assessing, and managing one's emotions. This capacity enables and empowers a person to cope better with life's challenges and the demands of work. Self-regulation is a lifelong struggle and a key component in the practice of diligence.

Daniel Goleman has popularized the theory with an Emotional Competencies model that highlights self-awareness and self-management.[3] Goleman points out that emotional competencies, or learned capabilities, must be developed to achieve outstanding performance. He identifies them as *impulse control*, *understanding*, *persistence*, *zeal*, and *self-motivation*, clearly all necessary for the practice of diligence and in need of an early start.

Emotional intelligence is a crucial component in the development of diligence, because emotional control counters the impulse to give up.

MIDDLE CHILDHOOD: *Room for Improvement*

Between ages seven and twelve, children appreciate that persistence pays off but has a certain cost. It means that it usually takes more time and more patience to finish a homework assignment, master a play in sports, perfect a ballet step, or meet Mom's standards for cleaning up! Significant developmental tasks during middle childhood are the attainment of competence and confidence, both of which fortify the habit of diligence.

Seven-year-old Ricci's high energy level usually placed our son either on a field or court. By excelling in sports, he derived satisfaction and built self-worth. While other children might have struggled to practice for hours at a time, Ricci found it easy and natural to persevere with his backhand strokes in tennis.

So it came as a surprise to our family when Ricci took an interest in stamps and coins, a rather sedentary hobby that requires considerable diligence to sort out a collection. His interest and curiosity were first piqued by the colorful stamps on envelopes arriving from distant lands and the coins given him by foreign visitors. He spent many hours organizing his collections into albums and started to read books for hobbyists. As the years passed, he persevered in his hobby; he found additional motivation when he realized that there was money to be earned in trading! But he also found that the 'down time' he spent on his hobby gave balance to his life.

After school, Grade 5 students Raoul, Peggy, Sanjay, Phil, and Laura met to talk about their homework assignment, a joint science project. Their discussion was lively; each had a different take on the project, but they finally agreed on how to approach their work.

Throughout the project, the teacher, Ernie, was struck by the differing degrees of diligence among the ten year olds. He observed that three demonstrated steady, earnest, and energetic application, whereas the other two executed their particular tasks half-heartedly, satisfied with mediocrity.

Noticeable differences between the two expressions of diligence follow.

When students practice diligence, they exercise the following...	When students exercise a lack of diligence, they demonstrate...
■ compliance with the rules of the project	■ unwillingness to tolerate obstacles in the project
■ independence in execution of tasks	■ resistance to suggestions for changes
■ appreciation for the teacher's supervision and suggestions	■ some defiance when a task needs to be redone
■ follow-up	■ complaints about the effort required to finish
■ attention to details and quality work	■ satisfaction with mediocrity
■ determination to finish	
■ positive responses to encouragement	

Experienced parents, caregivers, and teachers recommend strategies to nurture the exercise of diligence in the elementary years.

Opportune Moments

To foster diligence in Middle Childhood (7–12 years)

- Encourage a continuing sense of awe and discovery in learning, whether in the domains of academics, hobbies, or sports, in order to motivate diligence in a wide range of activities and interests.

- Guide the child to appreciate that learning and studies require continuing good work and perseverance. Repetition of drills and exercises requires fortitude to complete tasks.
- Set high but reasonable, realistic standards and expectations for each child.
- If possible, provide a work place (a desk or quiet corner of a room) where the child can do homework assignments and projects without the distractions of media. This will motivate concentration and the establishment of 'down time.'
- Remind the child that patience is a virtue and a deciding factor which facilitates attainment of goals. Strong determination is a must.
- Encourage the child to pay attention to accuracy and precision in work, e.g., penmanship, accuracy of content, details.
- Supervise homework assignments without interference; this dissuades dependency behavior or intellectual laziness.
- Emphasize the importance of reading instructions carefully.
- Firmly establish the priority of work over media use, e.g., computer games.
- Exercise parental media management to create a balance between the child's work and media use. Establish and explain family rules and criteria.
- Guide the child to gain impulse control and resist the temptation of immediate gratification.
- Delegate increasingly more difficult household chores as the child matures. Demonstrate the chores. Thank the child for his or her participation in household management; participation fosters family unity.
- Challenge the child to think of more creative and efficient ways of doing chores.
- Suggest that while doing chores with siblings, the children sing songs, do rhymes, or play word games.
- Minimize excessive competition, especially among siblings, lest it promote favoritism, resentment, and demoralization among sisters and brothers.
- ROLE MODEL DILIGENCE.

A Problem in the Process: Computer Game Addiction

"To the future generations of youth who never saw a world without the Internet, never had a home without TV, never lived a day before the cell phone, never handled a research project without Google—who teaches them how to navigate this unprecedented explosion of options?"[4]

Who, indeed, keeps our youth on track and guides them in the habit of diligence, i.e., stopping, starting, or continuing what they are supposed to be doing, namely their work of play, study, chores, hobbies, or sports? Who helps them conquer addictions that may develop in the course of playing computer games?

Addictive behavior is "nearly always in reaction to being emotionally stressed; this requires understanding of how it works psychologically."[5] Behavioral indicators include unhealthy compulsions that show themselves in psychological dependence or intense cravings.

Joey, an eleven year old, is a loner and bored at school. He shows increasingly less interest and more difficulties in his school work, probably because of his preoccupation with playing computer games. He finds relief here from his loneliness, stress, and school pressure but is unable to discipline himself. Lately, his parents notice that Joey makes excuses to be absent from class and has given up his favorite sport, skateboarding.

Computer games and "online gaming habits have crossed over from a hobby into an addiction. Six main areas are often affected by computer game addiction: (1) psychological and emotional with a higher risk of experiencing self-esteem problems, depressed mood, social anxiety, and mood instability. Addicts may feel guilty and ashamed for not being able to control their habits; (2) health; (3) family life; (4) finances; (5) academics; and (6) socialization."[6]

Research indicates that 8.5 percent of American youths between eight and eighteen become "pathological gamers." They do worse in school and have trouble paying attention in class, and are twice as likely to manifest attention-deficit hyperactivity disorder. Boys are four times more likely to become addicted than girls; the vulnerable stage for addiction to begin appears to be between eight and nine years of age.[7]

Several symptoms should alert parents, caregivers, and teachers to potential addictions:

- Spending increasing amounts of time and money on video games in order to feel the same level of excitement
- Irritability or restlessness when play is scaled back
- Escaping problems through video play
- Skipping homework to spend more time at the controller
- Lying about the length of playing time
- Stealing games or money to play more.[8]

Playing computer games can be a great source of entertainment, fun, learning, and socialization among children, but it can also evolve into a dreaded obstacle with the potential of sorely undermining the development of diligence in the work of children. Addicts prefer their compulsive game play to worthwhile activities such as studies, hobbies, sports. Parents are advised to exercise parental media management, i.e., set time limits; locate the computer in a public place in the home; monitor the content and values projected in the games; engage in interactive play; and exercise restrictions. Should addictions develop, consultation with a school guidance counselor or a qualified professional psychologist is advisable.

Adolescence: *Best Efforts*

Adolescence is characterized by changes in the physiological, emotional, cognitive, social, and moral-spiritual domains of development. Physically, the teenager experiences hormonal and growth spurts and maturation of the reproductive organs. Emotionally, mood swings, self-doubts, and insecurities kick in. Cognitively, the adolescent is capable of more abstract and analytical thinking. The search for identity begins. The teenager demonstrates more assertion of independence and freedom. Socially, he/she must cope with fears of nonacceptance and peer pressure. Moral choices between right and wrong and questions about the ultimate purpose of life beg for answers.

In a nutshell, basic developmental tasks require adolescents to learn how to: be oneself, prove oneself, make up one's own mind, take responsibility for oneself, be successful, and love and be loved—all formidable challenges on the journey to maturity.

Some teens make the transition with ease while others do not. A host of factors could account for their difficulties. Among the more recently identified are "dramatic changes in brain structure involved in emotions, judgment, organization of behavior, and self-control that take place between puberty and young adulthood."[9] These changes may partially explain the adolescent's difficulty with impulse control, instinctual reactions, reckless behavior, and inability to sustain school work.

Thoughtful recommendations from parents, caregivers, and teachers foster diligence in teenagers.

Opportune Moments

To foster diligence in Adolescence (13–19 years)

- Respect the dignity of the teenager by treating him/her with good manners.
- Guide the teenager's pursuit of individual talents. This respects his/her sense of individuality.
- Find accomplishments to praise so that the adolescent believes in him/herself and develops self-confidence.
- Encourage the teenager to formulate a motto about finishing what has been started or suggest a clever one.
- Guide the adolescent towards ethical standards in studies, sports, hobbies, projects.
- Motivate the pursuit of excellence as a standard for work.

- Guide the teenager in his or her impulse control and self-regulation.
- Encourage emotional intelligence, i.e., determination and persistence in any task.
- Encourage thoughts and plans about the future.
- Elicit thoughts about how to attain future goals. Make suggestions without dictating choices. Self-motivation is a key factor.
- ROLE MODEL DILIGENCE.

....

A Problem in the Process: Lack of Motivation

Among the internal problems during adolescence that may stand in the way of diligence are laziness, low self-worth, insecurities, and lack of motivation.

Motivation is both an external and internal process that activates, guides, and sustains behavior over time. It is the reason why people behave the way they do and reflects energized, directed, and sustained activity.

Lack of motivation comes into focus in the following educator's experience with a teenager in early adolescence.

Gerard O'Malley, Ph.D, a retired New Jersey assistant superintendent of schools, relates his attempt at motivating a student. As a young teacher, he guided a thirteen year old in his English class.

"Peter was bored with school and made only superficial efforts to complete assignments. Any task requiring original thinking, thoughtful consideration, or a reasonable amount of concentration was not worthy of his time and effort.

"One day I gave an open-ended assignment to write three paragraphs about anything of interest. I gave the class several examples of topics that could be used and provided time to complete the assignment. After a short period of time, I noticed that Peter had not written anything, so I asked if I could help. He replied with an emphatic no, and explained he had given up because he just didn't do anything worth writing about.

"I knelt down next to his desk and began telling about my experiences with not knowing what to write, but he said he just didn't want to think any more about it. However, I was persistent and asked him to tell me what he did after school. He said that he didn't do anything, but slowly and grudgingly proceeded to account for his activities in detail.

"Somewhere in the process of responding, he mentioned going to his boxing lesson. I said that was very interesting, and although I didn't know very much about boxing, I might like to learn. I told him a friend used the term 'right cross' while telling me about a boxing match and wondered what it is. He was surprised by my lack of knowledge and that I might be interested in learning something from him. Slowly and patiently he proceeded to enlighten me, and one thing led to another until he became engrossed in his explanations of other terms commonly used in boxing.

"When Peter finished, I said, 'Why don't you write about what you just told me?' He was surprised that his knowledge of this subject would be appropriate for the assignment and proceeded to place his thoughts on paper. The end result was a logical step-by-step story related to his boxing experience.

"When I returned his paper and congratulated him on a fine piece of writing, I asked him what he learned from the experience. He said he was surprised at how much he knew about boxing and that others would be interested in learning about what he knew. We talked about the need for determination and perseverance in the boxing ring and that a boxer must think about many different strategies to be successful. He strongly agreed, and then we talked about how these applied to his assignments and other experiences he had. It was obvious that he was proud of his accomplishment.

"Much to my delight, he seemed to acquire more confidence in his ability to explore ideas and share them with others. This was evident in the quality of subsequent assignments and the success he had in other subjects. His attitude seemed to change, and he began to be more social with other students."

With depth and wisdom, Dr. O'Malley further analyzed in six steps Peter's change in behavior and his early experience at developing the virtue of diligence:

1. An adult recognized him as an individual and showed respect for his thoughts, interests, and activities.
2. Peter was helped to realize that his thoughts were valued and that he had knowledge and skills others did not have.
3. He learned that his contributions had value in a setting among his teachers and his peers.
4. He acquired a respect for his thoughts and the confidence and determination to use them to complete a task.
5. His learning was reinforced by an opportunity to examine it and articulate what he had learned.
6. He was able to transfer some of the personal attributes required by a successful boxer to his own personal development.

Here is a poignant example of a young teacher who was able to inspire a teenager to internalize short- and long-term intrinsic factors of motivation: interest, joy, eagerness, readiness, self-mastery, and the will to use freedom wisely to choose one's own destiny.

In developing diligence, extrinsic factors also successfully motivate children, e.g., grades; rewards; meaningful subject matter; interesting, challenging teaching strategies; springboards, projects or assignments; and a parent's or teacher's personality, interest, role modeling, and encouragement. Clearly the teacher played a pivotal role in Peter's story by giving him an experience of success that strengthened self-worth and confidence.

Quotables: *Diligence*

Work and work-related virtues have inspired many noteworthy personalities to share their insights. The reader is invited to add a personal reflection culled from experience. Following are several quotations related to the virtue of diligence.

1. "All labor that uplifts humanity has dignity and importance and should be undertaken with painstaking excellence."[10]
2. "Have you seen how that imposing building was built? One brick upon another. Thousands. But one by one. And bags and bags of cement, one by one. And blocks of stone, each of them insignificant compared with the massive whole. And beams of steel. And men working, the same hours, day after day. Have you seen how that imposing building was built? By dint of little things!"[11]
3. "I know the price of success: dedication, hard work, and an unremitting devotion to the things you want to see happen."[12]
4. My thoughts:

CHAPTER 2

LAUNDRY DAY: *Order in Work*

MONDAY: *A Good Start*

Like clockwork, Mama reserved Mondays as laundry day, a time set aside to do the family wash. It was a predictable, orderly routine that played out each week among the housewives of Fern Avenue.

Mama approached laundry day with precision and order. And as a four year old, I felt privileged to be her partner in the process.

First on the agenda, we gathered the soiled laundry. With two large wicker baskets in hand, Mama and I emptied the hampers of soiled laundry and sorted out the pieces according to color.

I remember how Mama purposely soaked red socks in a basin of water and waited until the liquid turned bright pink. She wanted to demonstrate how noncolorfast clothes may fade. Then she asked me what might happen if she put my white blouse into the water... deep thinking for a four year old.

We owned an old fashioned ringer-type washing machine, unlike any of the modern machines, but it did an adequate job and saved considerable time. We did not own a clothes dryer, so the wash had to be hung in our garden... but only after the clothes lines had been wiped clean!

Sequencing the order in which the laundry was hung was in itself an art and a science. The clean, wrung laundry was sorted out according to sheets and towels. Clothing was classified into categories of underwear, socks, and shirts and hung together. Perhaps without realizing it, Mama was teaching her young daughter a systematic, scientific approach to the mundane task of laundering. In effect, I was learning logical, sequential, and consequential thinking! We followed the same routine every week, except if it rained or snowed. In that case, we hung the wash in the basement of our home and followed an alternative plan.

When the laundry was dry, the process reversed itself. We methodically took down the laundry from the lines according to category, folded the pieces, and neatly stacked them into the wicker baskets for return to the right drawer or closet. I will not go into the next phase of laundering: ironing. That's a whole other story!

Monday was an ordinary day for most young children. But for me it was extraordinary. It meant that I got to spend a morning with Mama listening to her anecdotes about growing up in turn-of-the-century Germany. More than her story-telling, Mama's clear approaches and instructions in laundering were a bonus. They paved the way for habits that I would carry into my own household.

....

A word of explanation may be in order. Some unwritten laundering rules governed housewives in the 1940s and 1950s. The first among many dictated that laundry day had to be Monday. What better way to start the week! Other logical ones followed naturally: white wash must be washed separately from the colorful pieces lest the colors run and ruin a favorite dress. Sheets were hung on the perimeter of the drying area to hide underwear from public view! Clothespins were used to speed drying. Men's shirts were always hung with clothespins by their tails, not at the shoulders.

Laundry day required methodical procedures for efficient completion. A special treat awaited families on Monday; there was nothing quite like the scent of sheets newly harvested from clothes lines!

Order Defined

Order is a good habit or virtue that is essential to a given task or plan. Order puts direction and purpose into an activity, assignment, or procedure. It requires a multipronged plan of action: a logical approach to a task, preparation for execution, punctual implementation, and continuous follow-up and follow-through.

Order is practiced in collaboration with other habits to bring a plan to completion, such as,

- Understanding or comprehension and appreciation
- Prudence or sound judgment and conscience
- Temperance or self-control and self-regulation
- Responsibility or accountability for thoughts, words, actions
- Justice or equitableness and lawfulness
- Punctuality or strict observance of an appointed time or keeping of appointments
- Precision or accuracy and exactness
- Patience or uncomplaining endurance

The exercise of these virtues goes hand-in-hand with the practice of order.

If the habit of order is not developed steadily from the earliest years, repercussions can be long lasting. Among the components required to implement order are: a ***plan, direction, system, schedule, routine, priorities, management***, and ***limitations***. What happens when they are not in place?

Components of Order

When there is no ***plan*** or scheme that provides the **design** of the task or project, then children perceive no discernible course of action.

When there is no ***direction***, there is no reference point towards which the activity, task, or work aims. Children do not see the **purpose** of their work and may fall into rambling aimlessness. In the process, they may get demoralized and not finish. They may fail to see the importance of individual work that makes a contribution to coordinated efforts and the entire project.

When there is no ***system*** or systematic way of doing things, i.e., no 'modus operandi,' there is no **orderly sequencing** of tasks or arrangement of steps that will help children develop logical and consequential thinking.

When there is no ***schedule*** or **timetable**, there is no sense of timing for the completion of a task. Children may not see the need for punctuality and self-discipline to finish a project; they waste time in the process.

When there is no ***routine***, consistency, and **predictability**, children become unsettled, disoriented, and insecure.

When there are no ***priorities***, i.e., events or tasks do not follow one another in **order of importance**, then children may not be able to identify or discern what is of greater value or urgency. They may tackle a task hit or miss, trial and error.

When there is no ***management***, there is no **control** or regulation of the activity. No one takes charge or oversees the progress of a task. Children may not learn how to obey, regulate, and sustain their work.

When there are no ***limitations*** and **respect for authority**, children may not appreciate the boundaries or restrictions of behavior that will facilitate completion of a job; they may not strengthen their self-control over impulses and emotions. Without respect for authority, they lose the opportunity to learn from effective role modeling and leadership.

In sum, when the components of order are unregulated or left to chance, confusion, unrest, instability, or chaos may follow. Worry, demoralization, and lack of control are natural extensions of a wayward task. Training is therefore of the essence.

Fast Forward

From my simple story about how I learned lessons in the orderly process of laundering in the 1940s, I fast forward now to a very different scenario. The year is 1992. I have a fifteen-year-old son, Anton.

From my perspective, the music that was blaring couldn't really be called music. For someone who had been raised on Rogers and Hammerstein's musicals, I looked for a melody in every song. But my son's music didn't quite fit that mindset. Finally I commented, "Anton, I am having a hard time finding a melody in your music. It sounds more like noise to me."

"Mom, don't you realize that the music of my generation expresses the rage that we feel because of the chaos and disorder that your generation has introduced into this world?"

Chaos and disorder! I stood dumbfounded and astounded by the perception and sensitivity of my youngest. He had elevated the issue of order to a broader, global level and assigned accountability for the disorder.

Fast forward to 2012. The chaos has been compounded by more international political, economic, social, and moral upheaval amid natural catastrophes and environmental concerns. How do children who live in war-torn countries, calamity-stricken areas, abject poverty, societies riddled with corruption, or dysfunctional families make sense of disorder? We turn for some positive examples to the child's immediate world: the home and school settings.

The Home Setting

Even in a peaceful and orderly home environment, children are exposed to disorder when they view mayhem and uncertainty in news broadcasts and other television programs, computer games, films, and via the Internet. With a constant barrage of confusing concepts and frightening, chaotic images, they may grow to expect disorder as a normal backdrop to daily life; they may become desensitized to violence.

Whatever its constellation, the family is still the most natural setting, most basic social unit, and first cell of society. Whether children live in the 'city that never sleeps' or in a rural setting, they need to find in the family a source of clear direction and a haven of serenity. As the first school of life, the family counterbalances whatever discord children may witness elsewhere and teaches coping skills to help maintain equilibrium.

During good times, when daily life follows a predictable plan and schedule, children feel reassured and secure. But when crises, unexpected events, or changes occur, they react or overreact, perhaps confused, distrustful, and doubtful of solutions.

Families on overseas assignments for the military, government, or multinational corporations face unique challenges. Transplanted to new environments or cultures, parents must continue to provide order in family life. They need to involve the children in the move, e.g., pack and unpack; set up a household as soon as possible; continue to assign familiar chores; find suitable schooling; keep up with relatives and friends to fortify ties and provide continuity; and look for meaningful activities that will familiarize the family members with their new surroundings. Role-modeling of organization, perseverance, confidence, and optimism are essential to the parental role.

In an age when mechanization and small businesses relieve many people of household tasks, families are cautioned to find good uses for the spare time generated.

When Timmy's parents hired a gardening service, everyone in the family sighed with relief. It meant more leisure on Saturdays exempt from mowing the lawn, planting, watering flowers, pruning, and replanting in their suburban garden. During the first three weeks after the service had begun, everyone went their own way. By the third Saturday, however, they realized they were not using the extra time to build up their unity as a family; on the contrary, the family members were all doing their own media-based thing while missing the fun they had once enjoyed together.

Timmy, the youngest, surprised everyone with the suggestion that they go on weekly excursions to nearby parks. Older brother Stuart preferred family tennis. Seeking relief from the household routine, Mom wanted to visit malls and dine out. Dad just wanted to tinker with his car and teach his sons about auto mechanics and the fundamentals of driving. The family negotiated, compromised, and finally put together a plan for activities that would meet everyone's needs and restore family ties.

Even in the more informal setting of the family, the components of order are essential to unity.

The School Setting

In the more structured environment of school, children continue to internalize the meaning and application of order. In this socially expanded setting, good manners and right conduct become essential for classroom management and an atmosphere conducive to learning. Parents can considerably facilitate the work of teachers by training children from the youngest years on to wait their turn, listen, and not interrupt conversations. These seemingly small social gestures foster order and multiply time.

A veteran kindergarten teacher of thirty-four years, Sara incorporated all the components of order into any given class day. At the beginning of the day, she established a plan by explaining the schedule of activities; this concretized daily goals and a timetable, and fostered self-discipline to complete a task. To clarify matters, she allowed time for the children's questions, feedback, and repetition of instructions.

To understand the purpose of the work at hand, she explained each activity and the reason for doing the task; this gave direction and motivated the children to finish, e.g., "Your paintings will make the room look cheerful when they are hung"; or "Our bean seed will grow into food we can eat."

To prepare and execute a task with precision and punctuality, Sara guided the children in gathering all the materials needed for the activity. Sometimes she set a timer to give an auditory signal to stop. For follow-up and closure to the activity, she assembled the children and asked them to describe what they had done, what they liked about the activities, what was hard or easy, and what they had learned. If time allowed, each child showed what he/she had accomplished.

By establishing limitations and classroom management, Sara helped foster obedience and a sense of security. As a daily routine, the children experienced parameters and structure, an orderly system, and the priority of starting and finishing their work.

In sum, with an educational philosophy and system in place, the components of order find expression in the school setting.

Early Childhood: *Small Beginnings*

Renowned Italian educator Maria Montessori (1870–1952) maintained that children demonstrate a strong sensitivity to order. Starting at birth and peaking between eighteen months and two and a half years, this extraordinary sensitivity may extend to age five.

Characterized by "a desire for consistency and repetition there exists a passionate love for established routines. The 'terrible twos' are often exaggerated reactions to small disruptions in order, not usually perceived by adults. The environment therefore must be carefully ordered with a place for everything and with carefully established ground rules."[1]

Grandma Rita explained that her granddaughter, Vicky, had been trained at home to put her belongings in order. For example, at home she arranged her school shoes, dress-up shoes, ballet slippers, and sandals by lining them up in orderly rows for easy access. Somehow this external order led her to a sense of internal order.

When the family visited a shoe store in a mall, Vicky, almost two, was very disturbed by the disarray of shoes, many of them off their shelves, some on the floor, others out of their boxes. Very methodically, Vicky proceeded to put order into the shoe display. The sales personnel smiled and clearly appreciated her help!

Opportune Moments

To foster order in Early Childhood (3–6 years)

- Schedule play time together with the child during weekdays and weekends; however short the time may be, this fosters bonding between parent and child.
- If the child is working, don't interrupt the work cycle.
- Patiently explain how to do a task or play with a more complicated toy.
- Break down instructions step by step, e.g., how to build a toy bridge, do a jigsaw puzzle, a household chore.

- Repeat instructions until the child is able to begin and accomplish the activity or task on his/her own.
- Train the young child to establish a daily routine of putting things in their proper place, e.g., toys, books, clothes, shoes.
- Train the child to prepare his or her school bag and needed school items the night before class.
- In a relaxed and natural manner, patiently remind the child to do a chore without resorting to harsh punishments. If the child does not comply, impose a consequence, e.g., withdrawal of a privilege, and explain how the lapse in doing the chore brings disorder.
- Be consistent about corrections. This reassures the child about appropriate behavior.
- Make chore time a fun time with younger children. Capitalize on their eagerness.
- Thank the child for his/her help.
- Give the young child a sense of schedule, e.g., a daily time for eating meals, bathing, sleeping, playing, doing school assignments.
- Adhere to a schedule, emphasizing the importance of self-discipline and order to give direction to tasks.
- Establish time limits and a definite schedule for media use, e.g., television or video viewing, computer game play. Include reading as an exciting alternative.
- Limit the acquisition and use of technology, e.g., iPads, iPods, Nooks which are expensive, time-consuming, and distracting from work.
- To preserve order among siblings, schedule television viewing and use of other technology on a definite timetable so that each child gets his/her turn; this practice avoids bickering and promotes sharing and thoughtfulness. Enlist the children's suggestions and agreement to a plan.
- Despite protests or procrastination, encourage the child to stick to a predictable daily schedule and practice punctuality.
- ROLE MODEL ORDER.

A Problem in the Process: Noncompliance

With their capacity for self-regulation still minimal, children in early childhood have difficulty obeying directions and rules; they need limitations and opportunities to internalize a control system (see Chapter 1 "Lack of Self-Regulation").

Scott, almost three, was having a hard time. Eager to help but rebuffed by his busy mother at a time when she found his help inconvenient, or wanting to join older siblings playing a board game but told instead to get out of the room or else frustrated at not winning the game, he acted out through tantrums. Parental inconsistencies made him confused and defiant. At this age, the child feels out of control.

Scott needed a firm but loving hand to restore order in his behavior. Whatever the reasons for noncompliance, effective strategies usually incorporate (1) a distraction; (2) redirection to an alternative activity; (3) simply a firm 'no'; or (4) patience in cases of illness, fatigue, and hunger.

At school, the child may misbehave through physical aggression, e.g., hitting, pushing, pinching, grabbing, and biting; or he may shout, not share, or have difficulty accepting mistakes.

Several reasons account for the misconduct: a need for more attention, involvement, and independence, or the desire for revenge, justice, or power. Limits must be set to facilitate the child's compliance.

How can the child be guided effectively?

- State clear limits.
- State specific limits and rules.
- Phrase limits and rules in an impersonal way.
- Give limits and rules one at a time.
- When possible, state how the child can control him/herself within the limits.
- Maintain good eye contact with the child when speaking.
- When appropriate, give the child choices or options.

- Prioritize limits and rules, e.g., health, safety, routine and order in the home and school, playtime, school work, chores, care of property, good manners, kindliness.
- Repeat limits and rules.
- Encourage and praise the child for his/her efforts. [2]

The dynamic process of teaching the child about behavior that is right, good, acceptable, and appropriate is called discipline. Parents have a natural right to discipline children as an exercise of authority, influence, and control over them. In the absence of the parents, teachers have the right to act as substitute parents and discipline their pupils.

Discipline aims to develop self-regulation in the child. The process targets the following:

- Help the child understand what he/she is doing.
- Guide the child to do what is right, good, acceptable, and appropriate.
- Develop the habit of self-discipline.
- Foster the responsible use of freedom.

Children even in early childhood are capable of reasoning out and answering specific questions related to their behavior. For example, (1) let the child describe his/her version of the misconduct; (2) help the child to understand that his/her misconduct affects others or may hurt someone; ask him/her to describe how the victim might feel; (3) guide the child to own the misbehavior and apologize; (4) ask why the misbehavior is wrong; (5) insist on a better way of behaving.

Training is of paramount importance and must begin in the earliest years to facilitate self-control and restore order in the child's behavior.

Middle Childhood: *Room for Improvement*

By middle childhood, it is essential for the family to establish daily family schedules that revolve around mealtimes, parental work and school schedules, homework, after-school activities, chores, and weekend activities. With a routine in place, children know what to expect. In the absence of a predictable weekly and daily plan, children may flounder and not take their work very seriously. They may have difficulty with impulse control and bypass opportunities to develop competence and confidence.

In middle childhood, children have the capacity to put order into their thoughts, academic subjects, and personal belongings; they like to develop hobbies involving collections and classification. Each generation has developed its own series of collectibles: stamps, coins, stationery, sports cards, model figures, Nancy Drew or Hardy Boys books popular in the past, or the more contemporary collections of stickers, Pokemon cards, *Harry Potter* or *Diary of a Wimpy Kid* series, music videos, and computer games. Children at this stage find satisfaction in putting together related items and classifying them. It appears to give them psychic satisfaction and direction; much of the fun comes from the socialization they experience when they trade their collectibles.

Opportune Moments

To foster order in Middle Childhood (7–12 years)

- Encourage the child to establish his/her schedule.
- Discuss the schedule with the child and the rationale behind it.
- Suggest that the child could post clever reminders, e.g., charts, lists, post-its, about school assignments and chores.
- Establish policies about how, when, and where the child does homework.
- Consistently follow the established policies and schedules.
- Explain the advantage of doing things with logical sequencing, not impulsivity; it is better to go from the simple to the more complex, step by step; this may require patience and time to wait for results.
- Encourage the child to finish what he/she has started.

- Explain expectations and procedures; demonstrate a chore, if needed.
- Expect some complaints, resistance, and backsliding in chores. With good humor, remind the child that doing chores builds character!
- Establish sanctions if chores are not completed, e.g., withdrawal of a privilege.
- Expect to negotiate on occasion or show flexibility when a schedule changes or unexpected events intervene.
- Exercise parental media management to maximize productive, worthwhile multimedia use, e.g., television, computer games, videos, cell phones, Internet, social media like Facebook, Twitter.
- Require the child to practice basic manners, e.g., to wait one's turn, not squeeze in front of others, or interrupt another's conversation.
- Provide alternative activities to multimedia, e.g., board games, visits to a museum, zoo, aquarium, book store, sports events, music or dance recitals.
- ROLE MODEL ORDER

A Problem in the Process: The Overscheduled Child

In their eagerness to be good providers and give their children everything they never had, parents may tend towards hyper-parenting. Hyper-parenting is a style of child rearing usually found among middle- and higher-income parents who can afford to finance extra enrichment activities for their children.

Basically, hyper-parents project onto the child their own hopes, dreams, needs, or expectations; view education as a competition; make sacrifices of time, energy, and expense to fulfill their expectations; and overschedule the child in too many extra activities.

Believing that parents have the power and obligation to craft a perfect childhood, hyper-parents assert that 'winning is everything' in this electronically competitive world. They maintain (1) that parents must provide the possessions and enrichment activities to raise perfect children; (2) that the goal of childrearing is to raise children who will lead a life of fame and fortune; and (3) that parents are failures and children losers if the parents don't provide.[3] These assumptions, influenced by materialistic values, reflect a false concept of perfection and misguided, unrealistic goals of childrearing and parenting.

The disorder of hyper-parenting is expressed in the overscheduling of children in too many activities that distract them from a schedule which would permit them to do their work, spend free quiet time to unwind, and enjoy childhood. These overscheduled children are deprived of unstructured, therapeutic, imaginative, and creative playtime.

Usually the overscheduled child participates in several extracurricular activities at school; is enrolled in other activities outside school on weekdays and weekends; and is in after-school tutoring programs or is tutored on a one-on-one basis at home. Often hurried and pressured, the child can hardly catch his/her breath and is fatigued by the overloaded schedule.

Research indicates that this multitasking "to accomplish too many tasks at one time increases the likelihood of errors and actually lengthens the time it takes to complete any one single task. Studies on the working of the brain have shown that task-switching can create a sort of bottleneck effect as the brain struggles to determine which task to perform."[4]

Aunt Stella wanted to include her eight-year-old nephew, Howie, in an excursion with her own children so that the child could spend more time with his cousins. When she asked Howie, "Would you like to join Candy and Kurt for some rock climbing on Saturday?" Howie answered, "Oh, thank you Aunt Stella, but I am so tired from all my activities this week."

Some children get exhausted, overanxious, discouraged, or rebellious, while others handle the super-activity very well, depending on factors like temperament and motivation. Some become overachievers and others underachievers; some don't know how to handle free time and entertain themselves. Eventually, they feel overloaded, overwhelmed, pressured, stressed, or scrutinized.

Of course the activities may stimulate learning and focus interests. The children may acquire new skills, channel their energies, enjoy the activity, learn socialization skills, and develop a sense of responsibility. But the benefits usually are acquired at a cost.

Parents must consider the tradeoffs and balance the child's schedule to maximize benefits to the child. They can achieve this through careful selection of activities based on the child's interest and motivation. By limiting the number of extra activities and fostering a reasonable balance between school work, chores, activities, and media exposure, parents are in a better position to monitor the child's reactions and be sensitive to the tipping point and overload.

Under the additional pressure of doing well in school work, "the cost of this relentless drive to perform at unrealistically high levels is a generation of kids who resemble nothing so much as trauma victims. They become preoccupied with events that have passed—obsessing endlessly on a possible wrong answer or a missed opportunity. They are anxious and depressed and often self-medicate with drugs or alcohol. Sleep is difficult and they walk around in a fog of exhaustion. Other kids simply fold their cards and refuse to play."[5]

ADOLESCENCE: *Best Efforts*

If the groundwork for order has been laid, adolescents will likely cope more successfully with teenage turbulence. They will be better prepared to focus on essentials and manage a plan and schedule despite distractions arising from peers and media.

With the support and guidance of family, friends, and teachers, teenagers have better chances of overcoming obstacles and disappointments. If adolescents have absorbed a sense of family and personal history and developed positive self-identity, they are likelier to overcome self-doubts.

Inspired by an old television program, *Kids Say the Darndest Things*, I decided to keep a record of noteworthy quotations and funny anecdotes of each of our children. I wanted them to know themselves when they were between two and six years of age and develop an understanding of their emerging personalities, individuality, and uniqueness.

By late adolescence and young adulthood, they would occasionally ask, "Mom, do you still have all of our quotations and stories that you recorded when we were young? Would you please read them to us?" Delighted by the request, I readily dug them out of a filing cabinet.

They laughed and joked and appreciated glimpses into their early childhood.

For example, while our three older children, ages seven, nine, and eleven were watching a TV family program in which the mother had just delivered a baby, our youngest, Anton, age three, listened intently while his older siblings discussed childbirth. He quickly sought me out.

"Mommy, is it true that when I was born I had an extension cord?"

"Did I really ask that?" or "Wow, you haven't changed much," were their usual reactions to their personal histories.

Photos bring back memories of family life, special occasions, personal milestones, or just goofy facial expressions are the stuff of photos. As children mature into adulthood, they are eager to view photos, whether hard copies kept in albums or the latest Instagrams. Adolescence is a good stage to assign the task of consolidating and organizing family and personal photos. This is another way of honing a sense of order in teenagers.

MaryJane, mother of seven, remarked that among the most important items to salvage in case of fire or natural calamity are the photo albums or CDs that house the pictures. They are windows to the past and irreplaceable recordings of family history.

Opportune Moments

To foster order in Adolescence (13–19 years)

- Inspire teenagers in late adolescence to realize that education and learning never end; that the development of virtues is a life skill and a lifelong struggle.

- Tap the interests and talents of the adolescent; this motivates resourcefulness, imagination, creativity, and self-discipline to practice and perfect skills, keep to a schedule, and develop resourcefulness.
- Teach goal setting by making a daily and weekly plan. Train teenagers to make lists just like Grandma!
- When the adolescent is overwhelmed with a project or assignment, suggest that he/she break down the task bit by bit to avoid frustration or the temptation to give up.
- Periodically ask the teenager about his/ her progress or difficulties in achieving a plan or goal. This could open the door to fruitful discussions.
- Teach the teenager to establish a time-line to monitor progress of a project or talent.
- Encourage regular scheduling of sports, music, dance practice, or other activities; limit the number of extra activities.
- Suggest that the teenager get in the habit of using his/her cell phone as an alarm clock to provide reminders of things to do.
- Remind the teenager to be punctual in the submission of projects and assignments; explain that punctuality shows respect for others and the requirements of a task.
- If there is a change of plans, guide the teenager to reorganize or reschedule tasks.
- Establish routine household expectations, e.g., turn off lights, lock doors, check gas in the car, keep the car and house keys in a safe place, return car keys after use.
- Suggest that the adolescent label items, e.g., books, shirts, sports equipment.
- Establish rules about social life to put order and perspective into socialization, e.g., curfews or guidelines for going to parties, overnight stays, malls, and excursions. Require contact information about whereabouts and make clear the importance of keeping in touch.

- Continue to require that adolescents fulfill household chores. Role reversal at this stage is a possibility, e.g., let the teenager cook dinner while Mom is the assistant.
- Encourage journal writing to help the teenager put order and perspective into experiences and the personal journey toward maturation. Respect the privacy of the journal or diary.
- Respect the individuality of the teenager who is in the process of strengthening self-confidence. Affirm the choice of like-minded friends who have similar values and clear direction.
- ROLE MODEL ORDER.

A Problem in the Process: Distractions

Adolescents are disadvantaged by multiple distractions that mislead, waylay, deter, or undermine the pursuit of good work. Powerful messages tell them: "Happiness is attained mainly through the acquisition of goods," or "Your worth is measured by how much you own," or "You can't be happy unless you buy. "

There is nothing wrong in itself with having material things. They are simply means to ends. Complications arise when teenagers desire material things as ends in themselves. When they become excessively attached to their belongings, or flaunt them to gain popularity or prestige, or prioritize frivolity and escapism over prudence and self-discipline, they are manifesting a superficial value system. Such values dupe adolescents into thinking that progress and success lie essentially in acquisition of material goods, attainment of immediate gratification, and achievement without commensurate work. They get all too few messages telling them their true value is in who they are as persons, as measured by the virtues they practice.

The distractions of media factor heavily into adolescent's work and play. The remarkable technology that bombards adolescents must be reevaluated and kept under control. Unless parents, grandparents, and other caregivers take direct, active interest in encouraging and supervising alternative activities in music, dance, sports, reading, hobbies, and family excursions, media may dominate the leisure of teenagers. When they receive instant visual images, or are lured by pornography, or experience the excitement of gaming, or can interact 24/7 with their friends on Facebook, how can their work compete with the powerful attractions of technology?

When media-related activities are the main items on the teenager's schedule, parental media management must come into play. To ensure a healthy integration of both media and non-media activities, work takes priority. The work of teenagers is still school and homework, hobbies, sports, activities, and chores, successively supplemented by or integrated with media exposure.

Quotables: *Order*

1. "Orderliness is having a sense of where things belong and how they relate to each other, and keeping them organized accordingly. When there is a place for everything and everything in its place, then we are able to think and work efficiently."[6]

2. "Order is the sanity of the mind, the health of the body, the peace of the city, the security of the state. Like beams in a house, or bones in a body, so is order to all things."[7]

3. "Being busy does not always mean real work. The object of all work is production or accomplishment and to either of these ends there must be foresight, system, planning, intelligence, and honest purpose, as well as perspiration. Seeming to do is not doing."[8]

4. My thoughts:

CHAPTER 3

A WORKING MAMA: *Responsibility in Work*

Delegating Duties

After twenty-five years of loyal service as a tool and die maker, Papa didn't anticipate that his employer would go bankrupt in 1952. Conscientious and dependable, he embarked immediately on a job search. Meanwhile, our dear Mama recognized her responsibility to supplement the family income. She also welcomed an opportunity to start a career outside the home.

Mama applied for a sales position at Bamberger's Department store in Newark and got the job. We sisters were very proud of our Mama. She passed the job interview, revealed unforeseen talents, formed many friendships with colleagues, and best of all enhanced our wardrobes with some of her earnings!

Often, we took the bus to her workplace and observed her in action. Always ready with service and a smile, she was also quite convincing and persuasive during her transactions with customers. Beyond her enormous goodness, we now gained glimpses into Mama's shrewdness and professionalism. She had always wanted to study law, but times were hard in post-World War I Germany and she was not able to pursue further studies.

A model employee, Mama gave us our first lessons in how to harmonize home and career. She integrated two professions through her accountability to both. Somehow she still managed to sew, although on a more limited basis. The house was kept clean and home-cooked meals were always tasty and nutritious. This was possible because Mama recognized teachable moments for training us in the virtue of responsibility. By wisely delegating household chores early on, I learned how to iron and begin the dinner preparation because I was the first to return home each day. That always meant cooking some variation of potatoes; I learned seven ways in the process! Those experiences served us sisters well, a foretaste of responsibilities in running a household.

....

Not unlike the dilemmas that many families face in the new millennium, our family situation called for unity and responsibility during the transition from Papa's joblessness to employment. Meanwhile, Mama, our working mother, was enjoying her career and the chance to learn new skills. She remained in full-time employment until her mandatory retirement.

Responsibility Defined

Responsibility is a good habit that gets things done because of a keen sense of duty. When practiced, the virtue demonstrates accountability, fulfillment of obligations, and uprightness in the completion of one's work and in dealing with others.

Training in the habit of responsibility links with the exercise of dependability grounded in high principles and trustworthiness.

Responsibility coordinates with other habits to complete a task:

- *Understanding* or comprehension and appreciation
- *Prudence* or sound judgment and conscience
- *Reliability* or steadfastness
- *Justice* or equitableness and lawfulness
- *Patience* or uncomplaining endurance
- *Fortitude* or courageous perseverance
- *Self-control* or self-discipline.

These related habits integrate with responsibility to bring work to fruition.

A Formula for Responsibility

A Willing Child + Effective Child Rearing + Role Modeling + a Conducive Environment + Commitment = A Formula for the Exercise of Responsibility. Let's look at those elements one by one.

A Willing Child

A *willing child* presupposes that the child understands what responsibility is and makes sound judgments. With good thoughts fed to the willpower, the child exercises his capacity to make choices, execute decisions, and sustain actions through constant implementation and follow-up.

Strong will reflects continuous training in the formation of good habits which evolve into virtues that are performed easily, quickly, constantly, readily, and naturally. The potential to practice responsibility relies on a support system of parents, caregivers, and teachers. While training children, backsliding is possible and likely unless the struggle to exercise responsibility is courageously counteracted through guidance and encouragement. The struggle continues until the habit is in place to predispose its possessor to accountability, dependability, and the responsible use of freedom.

Freedom is not simply doing whatever one likes, without restrictions. Teenagers may fall into this trap of misinterpretation. On the contrary, true freedom is a sensitive power of the will to choose a goal and a course of action that will lead to good choices and actions.

Within a framework of upright moral values, the responsible use of freedom upholds the dignity of the child. Parents, caregivers, and teachers are tasked with helping the child respect rules, laws, and upright lawgivers while avoiding decisions based only on whims, emotions, coercion, pressure, deception, or other superficial reasons.

Effective Child Rearing

The exercise of parental authority ranges from permissive to authoritarian to democratic. The latter is the most effective style because it establishes parameters, rules, and structure, gives explanations to the child, allows for participation and dialogue, supplies feedback, and imposes sanctions when the child misbehaves.

More recent popular terminology supplies labels for extreme parenting styles. A *helicopter mom* is one who hovers and micromanages the child, monitoring his or her moves and spelling out everything, without encouraging discovery and self-discovery. Concerned, involved, but overprotective, the helicopter mom tends to smother and inhibit the child's drive to do things for and by him/herself. By doing so, she fosters dependency behavior and not the responsible use of freedom.

The other extreme is the *free-range mom* who gives freedom with minimal preparation or supervision. A 'free-range child' may learn early decision-making and confidence, but if the child has not been trained in how to protect against possibly dangerous situations, free-ranging may actually jeopardize his or her safety and well-being.

Neither extreme is effective in the long run. 'Helicoptering' does not allow the child to uncover capabilities and take responsibility for choices and actions; 'free- ranging' by a passive parent may push the child beyond reasonable expectations and boundaries.

Applied to the classroom, the 'helicopter teacher' is highly controlling and probably authoritarian. She underestimates the child's capacity to think and decide on his/her own. The 'free-range teacher,' who does not establish parameters and classroom management, may overestimate the child's ability to deal with freedom responsibly.

Effective parents, caregivers, and teachers question, motivate, and guide. They lay foundations, teach strategies, and strengthen skills. Neither pushy nor intrusive, they inspire self-mastery, guide reasonable choices, and, most important, do not allow the child to escape the consequences of actions.

Role Modeling

Children at all stages of development, especially the very young, tend to emulate and follow the actions and styles of their mentors. When parents, caregivers, and teachers set good examples, children witness right, good, appropriate, and reasonable thought and behavior.

When children observe role models who set poor examples, they may become confused, flounder in their behavior, or remain clueless about what to do. Not having observed role models worthy of imitation, their capacity to develop a sense of responsibility is undermined.

A Conducive Environment

When children are situated in a family or school environment in which they understand clearly defined rules, criteria, expectations, and consequences, they are likely to follow the accepted ways of doing things and take responsibility for their behavior. If they have like-minded friends and classmates who are accountable and trustworthy, they are positively influenced and tend to imitate their peer's behavior. If, however, they are in crisis and among peers with questionable values, they may veer into risky behavior and irresponsibility (see Chapter 4 "Peer Pressure").

If situated in new and unfamiliar environments, children need time to become adjusted, identify their roles, and decipher the accepted values and mores of the group. This can be unsettling and may account for a temporary lapse of sound judgment and self-control. They may actually backslide and adopt the negative behavior of the group. In that case parents, caregivers, and teachers need to provide counseling and redirection to lead them back to responsible behavior.

Commitment

Commitment means engaging oneself steadfastly and making reliable long-term promises. It can be to relationships in the family, school, or friends; it may mean involvement in a cause, project, or issue; it can mean determination to uphold moral principles. Whatever the commitment, considerable effort, fortitude, and dependability are required to carry it out.

Fast Forward

With complex issues confronting the family and child rearing, the internalization of responsibility faces new, unforeseen challenges.

In the midst of major influences like the breakup of family solidarity, economic crises, unemployment, materialism, consumerism, unprecedented technology, and the power of media, the home and school settings are still the first sources of learning.

The Home Setting

The formula for responsibility is constantly tested in the home setting. Here is an example of what happens when some of the components in the formula for responsibility are neglected.

After continuous pestering that included harping on her safety, Naomi, age twelve, finally convinced her parents, Sharon and Buddy, to buy her a cell phone. She was thrilled with her new acquisition but unwilling to exercise any restraint in its use. Instead, she participated in nasty gossip and spread false rumors about classmates.

Ineffective parenting compounded the problem. Sharon and Buddy failed to set rules for the positive use of cell phones. They

- set no financial limitations on its use
- established no criteria about why and when to text or call
- were oblivious to the possible transmission of negative messages, e.g., bullying, obscene photos
- did not monitor Naomi's use of her phone

Only when monthly bills mounted and Naomi's school work deteriorated did her parents realize that their daughter was misusing her cell phone privilege under the influence of her classmates' bad example.

Naomi's parents temporarily withdrew her cell phone until all of the above problems were corrected and they were convinced that their daughter was mature and responsible enough to handle a cell phone. They wisely coordinated with other parents and the school to form a united front for the positive use of technology.

Another problem arises in adolescence when parents do not establish curfew hours and guidelines for parties, going to malls, sleepovers, overnight trips, camping, and similar activities.

When an unwilling child who lacks commitment to reasonable practices is guided by negligent parents and under pressure from peers, responsible use of freedom is jeopardized.

The School Setting

On their own in the school setting, children are under new pressures. They are expected to adjust, perform, and account for school performance and behavior away from home. Following is an example of the formula for responsibility put into action at school.

Bright and motivated, Luke, age fourteen, did well in Loretta's German class. He made excellent progress during the first four weeks of the six-week cycle of foreign language learning until he broke his arm in a fight.

Disturbed by the news, Loretta formulated strategies to guide Luke to sustain his good work and sense of responsibility.

Using his handicap as an excuse, Luke unexpectedly declared that he would not be able to do written assignments or take tests. She reassured him this difficulty could be managed in such a way as not to upset the momentum of his good work. "We'll work around it," she told him. "I will meet with you after school to review your assignments and give you oral tests."

"But I will be in detention after school," he answered.

"No problem, I will clear it with the teacher on duty."

Sensing her genuine concern, Luke agreed to the plan and committed to finish the course.

On the last day of class, 'the Frau' told him, "If you put your mind to good work, you will be a real leader. You have the potential to be one."

This story is reassuring for what it says about student achievement, but what lies beneath counts even more. Luke grasped that someone believed in him and cared enough to go out of her way to keep him on track. He learned valuable lessons about the importance of perseverance in spite of obstacles or complications. Instead of giving up, copping out, or getting into more fights, he strengthened his habit of responsibility.

EARLY CHILDHOOD: *Small Beginnings*

"Can I really expect my four-year-old daughter to be responsible?" a young mother asked.

"Yes, and better start early to train her," a seasoned grandmother quickly volunteered at a parenting seminar.

Unless pampered, young children are usually eager to help, participate, and do their work. They need to channel their energy in positive directions on a regular basis.

That's how they build skills, habits, and self-confidence. Three-year-old Josh is eager to show his drawing to Mom or demonstrate to Dad how he rides a bike. In effect, Josh is broadcasting, "You see, I can do it." He is expressing ownership of his work, taking responsibility, and, of course, seeking approval and attention.

Parents and teachers are most effective when they respond with a combination of encouragement and appreciation.

Shielding a child from taking responsibility is a common mistake among parents. It may lead to dependency behavior, learned helplessness, and eventually a poor work ethic.

OPPORTUNE MOMENTS

To foster responsibility in Early Childhood (3–6 years)

- Guide the child to take the consequences of actions and performance at home and school. Inappropriate behavior should be corrected quickly to help the child see the cause and effect of misconduct.
- Teach the child the importance of caring daily for personal possessions and of accepting the consequences of a loss.
- Avoid replacing the lost articles quickly, if at all. This is a rather painful yet realistic lesson in the responsibility of ownership.
- Explain to the child why, even in a throw-away society, he/she should not waste things. Make it clear that material possessions need care if they are to last.
- Use charts, calendars, and stickers to record positive accomplishments.

- Allow the child to help care for pets in a simply way at home or school.
- Encourage the young child to care for the environment at home and school, e.g., by throwing trash into the proper receptacle or caring for plants or flowers.
- If the child scatters toys or school materials on the floor, let the child pick them up to teach responsibility for tidiness and caring for his/her belongings.
- Let an older child suggest classroom rules, subject to approval.
- Assign reasonable tasks for the child to do at school, e.g., line leader, calendar leader, snack helper.
- Remind the child that telling lies to avoid punishment is doing injustice to others who will be affected. It is important to admit wrongdoing.
- ROLE MODEL RESPONSIBILITY.

A Problem in the Process: Learned Helplessness

The problem of 'learned helplessness' is not usually foreseen en route to responsibility. Parents excuse children's inability to undertake or finish their work on the basis of their young age, fatigue, lack of understanding, temperament, lack of self-discipline, or learning disabilities, and these may play a role. Two examples illustrate long-term effects that impeded responsibility for self and others.

Leo, age six, was a sickly child, suffering mostly from asthma attacks brought on by severe allergies. Despite tutoring, he lagged behind his classmates in reading and math. As much as he tried, Leo couldn't catch up and became discouraged. Eventually he stopped trying and felt increasingly anxious. As the year progressed, Leo's frequent absences and repeated failures led to demoralization and school phobia. Leo was headed for 'learned helplessness,' a mental attitude reflecting the expectation that he could not do anything to solve his problem.

At age five, Rachel already showed signs of extreme dependency behavior. By not allowing her to do anything for herself, e.g., feed or dress herself, carry her school bag, take care of her toys and belongings, Rachel's affluent and mostly absentee parents, along with her nanny, unwittingly contributed to learned helplessness. Her caregivers did not foresee the short- and long-term effects.

Rachel, the girl born with a silver spoon in her mouth, eventually felt powerless, lonely, and shy because she could not cope with simple demands. Not having been trained to think and fend for herself, she was set up for failure. She had difficulty in overcoming her anxieties and sense of helplessness even in adult life. Rachel thought of herself as privileged and therefore beyond accountability. She manipulated others to do things for her and provoked resentment in her relationships.

The child whose development is thwarted through learned helplessness needs guidance that will:

- go back to the basics to help the child gain or regain necessary concepts and skills
- give opportunities to help the child prove him/herself
- empower the child to have experiences of success that will strengthen and restore self-confidence
- encourage the child to take responsibility for self and others.

Without remedial efforts, the child may turn to diversions or vices that enable him/her to avoid accountability. Depression may eventually set in.

Middle Childhood: *Room for Improvement*

In middle childhood, children need to exercise responsibility in several domains: responsibility to God, society, others. Here is a chart indicating appropriate age levels for each.[1]

Levels of Responsibility

Domain	Age
Service—accountability to others	12 years
Discipline—answerability to self	10 years
Morality—care for actions and attitudes in relation to God and society	8 years
Obedience—response to parents	6 years

Barriers to the development of responsibility indicate a lack of training and role-modeling. When children are spoiled, pampered, and overprotected, they are deprived of valuable opportunities to overcome individual weaknesses. When they don't see in their parents, caregivers, and teachers examples of how to think, talk, and act responsibly, they are further deprived of heroes who stand up for standards and ideals.

In their safe neighborhood, Rae and Bill encouraged their son to take on a paper route at the age of eleven. Bill devised a sled to hold the papers, with a tarp over it so that the papers could be delivered in rain, snow, sleet, or hail. The child also was taught to record his earnings in a ledger. When he had earned enough money, he bought his first two-wheeler for $250. Proud of his accomplishment, he went on to become a financial analyst. As an adult, he took cross-country trips by himself, rain, snow, sleet, or hail!

Opportune Moments

To foster responsibility in Middle Childhood (7–12 years)

- Let the child do things for and by himself to develop ownership of behavior, self-confidence, and accountability.
- Engage the child in problem-solving to help him or her think of remedies and solutions to problems or conflicts. This is one of the best ways to develop responsibility. Ask the child to rate how he/she is doing.
- Remind the child about the importance of completing assignments and meeting deadlines before playtime.
- Beware of signals of school phobia and excessive excuses which may be symptomatic of fears of inadequacy or avoidance of responsibility.
- When tutoring or helping the child with homework, projects, music, or sports, avoid showing impatience or frustration. This will discourage the child, undermine self-confidence, and deter him/her from accountability.

- Explain the importance of taking responsibility for behavior and not covering up or blaming others. The latter behavior is dishonest and the easy way out.
- Encourage an environmentalist mentality to foster care for the planet and one's own immediate space.
- Let the child care for pets to foster dependability, e.g., walk the dog, feed the fish.
- Encourage the child to help take care of the simple needs of the very young and the aged, e.g., younger siblings or grandparents.
- If appropriate and safe, let the child buy basic groceries in a nearby store. Guide the child to count the proper change.
- Encourage the child to call a classmate who is sick and absent from school.
- Explain that it is rude to interrupt others or disturb their concentration and work cycle; such behavior can distract them from fulfilling their duties.
- At school, encourage each student to take responsibility for classroom cleanliness and tidiness.
- If the child makes a mistake, guide him/her to admit the mistake, rectify, and express regrets.
- ROLE MODEL RESPONSIBILITY.

A Problem in the Process: Dependency Behavior

Maria Montessori, the educator whose pedagogical methods reflect an astute appreciation of the nature of the child, reminded caregivers not to do for the child what he/she can do for him/herself. She maintained that children are capable of doing focused work and assuming responsibility for tasks and outcomes.

By middle childhood, the child should steadily be growing in accountability for work. An updated study in 2009 sheds light on the opposite, dependency behavior. The research aimed to discover why children from American middle-income families depend on their parents to do things for them. Undertaken by Dr. Elinor Ochs and other researchers at UCLA's Center on Everyday Lives of Families (CELF), the research studied families at home "to better grasp how families with two working parents balance child care, household duties and career, and how this balance affects their health and well-being."[2]

Thirty-two Southern California families who owned their own homes and had two to three children, with at least one between seven and twelve years, were video recorded for a week during almost every minute of the day. The footage was carefully analyzed and yielded the following findings.

- The families had a very child-centered focus, which may help explain the 'dependency dilemma.'
- Parents intend to develop their children's independence, yet raise them to be relatively dependent, even when the children have the skills to act on their own.
- Parents did most of the housework and indulged children.[3]

It appears that children were not asked to do tasks by the parents; instead, the children asked the parents to do work for them. The children were not empowered to exercise responsibility. In effect, parents provided service to children, and children consumed the service.

Significantly, the research indicated that "the children didn't seem to view it as their routine responsibility to contribute; in about 75 percent of the families, the mothers came home first and began to 'gyrate' through the house, bounding between the kids and their homework, groceries, dinner, and laundry."[4]

Parents who consistently do for the child what the child can do for him/herself are setting up the child for dependency behavior, laziness, passivity, and an unwillingness to take the initiative. By relinquishing parental authority and not requiring the child's participation, parents also set themselves up for exhaustion. Parents need to make a paradigm shift, from being overly accommodating and indulgent to being authoritative; they should not hesitate at all to require responsibility.

ADOLESCENCE: *Best Efforts*

Rae had a problem. Her sixteen-year-old son took a job to earn enough money for a class ski trip. He had agreed upon conditions with his parents and earned the needed amount. Shortly before the trip, he violated a crucial condition. When his parents learned of his misconduct, they knew they had to teach him a lesson in responsibility and remove the privilege of going on the trip.

When Rae informed her son of the parental decision, he was very disappointed and sad. But she wouldn't back down, lest her son be taught a negative lesson about the importance of keeping his promises and lose respect for parental authority. Rae admitted later that she had cried in silence. But because parental example and expectations were consistently implemented and taught, her son learned valuable lessons about trustworthiness and respect for oneself and others.

Lianne, mother of a young professional basketball player, traced the development of responsibility in her son, Chris, now in young adulthood. Her story reflected simple, consistent, and effective parenting techniques that strengthened habits into virtues.

A predictable school–homework–activity schedule was established in the earliest years. A consistent honor student, Chris was active as a class officer. With only a limited allowance and without the latest technology, he learned simplicity and restraint.

Although Chris engaged in the arts (e.g., piano playing and painting), he also tried his talents in several sports, like swimming, badminton, and golf. His height made him a natural for basketball, which he pursued in high school and college, playing on the varsity team in both. The long hours of practice toughened his resolve, developed good sportsmanship, and paved the way to responsibility.

Opportune Moments

To foster responsibility in Adolescence (13–19 years)

- Help teenagers to understand the true meaning of freedom. Establish guidelines and rules, set reasonable expectations, and give opportunities to test the waters. In the process, provide guidance that develops responsibility.
- Try to get to know your teenager's friends and classmates. This will give insights into potential peer pressure.
- Explain sanctions for misconduct and let the adolescent take the consequences of actions.
- Monitor the adolescent's established good habits, e.g., in studies, chores, hobbies, sports, music, dance, or care for the environment.
- Continue to monitor and manage media exposure by putting controls on the amount of time, kinds of programs, and media exposure of the teenager.
- Train teenagers to exercise restraint, respect, and responsibility in matters of human sexuality; block their exposure to media that flaunt promiscuity and pornography that disrespects human sexuality.
- Enroll teenagers in well-supervised summer programs to foster independence, skills, and socialization.
- Encourage them to get summer jobs to teach skills, accountability, and the value of money and savings.
- Elicit help in caring for the computer, e.g., repairs, replenishing ink and copy paper.
- Guide adolescent daughters and sons to care for personal hygiene and health; remind teenagers to take vitamins and medications, as necessary.
- Elicit help from teenagers to care for younger siblings; be vigilant that the teenager does not pass off his/her chores to the younger sibling.
- Respect the dignity of the adolescent. Self-respect and self-worth underlie the practice of responsibility.
- ROLE MODEL RESPONSIBILITY.

A Problem in the Process: Poor Work Ethics

Achieving a positive work ethic occurs over time. If the young child has gradually (1) come to understand the meaning, purpose, and value of work, (2) engaged in worthwhile activities of play, school work, chores, hobbies, sports, or music, and (3) been guided by role models worthy of imitation, the child has started to build solid foundations. But the internalization of a work ethic goes beyond just understanding, doing, and witnessing.

Work ethics are the concrete application of values that guide the child to see the dignity and nobility of human work and the importance of working by an ethical code. The latter is an objective measuring rod of moral standards that inspires integrity and excellence in work. Six **core moral values** ground the teenager in what is right and good: *love of God*; *respect for authority*; *selfless love for people*; *respect for the dignity of human sexuality*; *respect for truth*; and *responsible dominion over material things.*[5] These values are rooted in human nature, which has the capacity to seek truth and do good.

The process of internalizing work ethics can go either way—in the direction of honorable, upright, and noble work performed diligently, in a orderly manner, responsibly, cooperatively, and cheerfully; or it can take the opposite route of inept, sloppy, immoral performance, undertaken in a lazy, chaotic, unreliable, uncooperative, and negative manner.

The six core moral values prescribe a code of ethics for teenagers. Among possible transgressions are laziness, lying, lack of punctuality, disrespect for and disobedience to an authority figure, gossiping and slandering, cyber-bullying, stealing, extortion, drug and alcohol abuse, and promiscuous sexual behavior. All of these misbehaviors distract from the adolescent's work at hand.

At school, the teenager faces temptations to other specific violations. Among the most common are cheating on tests, plagiarism of reports and research papers, disrespect for the teacher or classmates, or foul play in sports.

The ethically upright teenager who upholds a code of work ethics:

- Respects the dignity of others
- Upholds the six core moral values
- Accepts the consequences of actions
- Practices work-related virtues
- Complies with school policies and rules
- Respects school property
- Exercises fairness to others

When ethical practices are well-grounded in a moral code, teenagers are on their way to exercising integrity or moral uprightness. This will serve them well as they undertake adult work in whatever capacity.

QUOTABLES: *Responsibility*

1. "If you want children to keep their feet on the ground, put some responsibility on their shoulders."[6]
2. "You must take personal responsibility. You cannot change the circumstances, the seasons, or the wind, but you can change yourself. That is something you have charge of."[7]
3. "It is easy to dodge our responsibilities, but we cannot dodge the consequences of dodging our responsibilities."[8]
4. My thoughts:

CHAPTER 4

A SUMMER BLOCK PARTY: *Cooperation in Work*

Neighborhood Solidarity

In the 1940s and 1950s outbreaks of polio threatened neighborhoods. Ours was not spared. Jules, the boy next door, was one of its victims. And so we sisters experienced what it meant to be put under quarantine. To contain the disease, travel beyond our street was restricted.

When the quarantine was lifted, the neighborhood mothers joined forces and organized a fund-raising activity to help support Sister Kenny, an Australian nurse who pioneered in efforts to develop rehabilitative therapy for polio.

"Everyone Welcome! Come out for an enjoyable evening to a show given by the children of Fern Avenue!" So read the flyer that circulated in our extended neighborhood. On two grueling hot summer evenings, July 20–21, 1950, we experienced true solidarity for the common good.

The show put on by us children featured instrumentals, solo and group chorals, and dancing, mostly hulas! Games and booths selling tasty home-cooked food and baked goodies highlighted the festivities.

Mama was an active force on the committee that organized the event, assuming her usual role on the refreshment committee. Her reputation as a great cook had preceded her. Again she showed us how to cooperate and work hard to achieve a noble purpose.

The two evenings were magical for us children; the fund-raiser generated tangible excitement and generous donations. Through cooperation, we united our efforts to pull off an activity that supported a worthy cause and contributed to the common good. And in time, we delighted in the news that neighbor Jules had made a complete recovery.

Cooperation Defined

Social beings are in need of others to help them grow, develop, improve, and attain self-actualization. To achieve these ends, cooperation is a vital component in the process.

Cooperation signifies working together for mutual benefit. It reflects a willingness to associate with and adapt to others to attain a goal. It reflects a spirit of collegiality and service that seeks the welfare of an individual or group, or the common good of society. Before objectives are met, the process of exercising cooperation may involve conflict, rivalry, and dissension, but teamwork manages to pull efforts together through negotiation and compromise, as necessary.

Cooperation can spell the difference between projects that work and projects that fail; relationships that are healthy or toxic; sports events that end in victory or loss; medical discoveries that promise cures or never fulfill expectations.

Social beings who unite and collaborate need to practice numerous related virtues to strengthen and enhance cooperation and a spirit of service:

- Humility or truthfulness about oneself; selflessness
- Respect or esteem and regard for the dignity of the other person
- Justice or equitableness and lawfulness
- Prudence or sound judgment and conscience
- Understanding or discovery of meaning in experiences
- Temperance or self-control and self-regulation

- Patience or uncomplaining endurance
- Fortitude or courageous perseverance
- Diligence or persevering effort
- Responsibility or accountability for thoughts, words, actions
- Optimism or hope for the best; looking at the bright side of things
- Cheerfulness or joy of spirit and optimism

The practice of these virtues contributes in one way or another to cooperative efforts.

Social Intelligence

Beyond emotional intelligence or EQ (the capacity for impulse control, self-motivation, self-management, and persistence—the qualities that foster diligence in work), Daniel Goleman explores social intelligence. Goleman asserts that human beings have a built-in bias toward empathy, cooperation, and altruism, provided they possess the developed *social intelligence* to nurture these capacities in themselves and others.[1]

Based on his research, Goleman concludes that "neuroscience has discovered that our brain's very design makes it sociable, inexorably drawn into an intimate brain-to-brain linkup whenever we engage with another person.... The more strongly connected we are with someone emotionally, the greater the mutual force. Our most potent exchanges occur with those people with whom we spend the greatest amount of time day in and day out, year after year—particularly those we care about most."[2]

If the child is to acquire the essential virtue of cooperation in and through his work, then parents, caregivers, and teachers are the most natural guides.

Fast Forward

From the simple summer block party of yesteryear to the complexities of socialization among youth in the new millennium, technology is clearly a major player in developing the virtue of cooperation.

At three and a half, granddaughter Maya started getting the hang of using a cell phone, even if it was only a soft-cloth toy given for her birthday. She enjoyed mimicking how grown-ups chatted over the phone. She surprised everyone when she requested that no one disturb her when she received calls (on her toy cell phone)! Maya pretended to have multiple conversations with family and friends and even put her callers 'on hold' as she pursued chats with at least four different parties! We can only assume that she was fostering cooperative efforts among her callers. Now seven, Maya is adept at texting when allowed to use her parents' cell phones.

For this generation of children, socialization has been accelerated by unprecedented media technology that can foster or hinder cooperation. Research shows both positive and negative findings.

On the one hand, "studies on the effects of Internet use in the 1990's and early 2000 showed that adolescents who spent a lot of time on the Internet spent less time with friends (Nie 2001), had fewer friends (Mesch 2001), and showed reduced social connectedness and well-being (Kraut et al. 1998)."[3]

Recent studies indicate more positive results for social networking. "Online communication stimulates rather than reduces social connectedness (Kraut et al. 2001). One study determined that the number of months a person is active on Twitter and the more hours per week he or she spends tweeting are positively related to camaraderie and connection to an online community (Chen 2010)."[4]

Although updated studies tend to reveal positive effects, the jury is still out. Time and more research will confirm or negate the benefits of social networking in the development of cooperation among children.

The Home Setting

Whether a family is small or large, the home setting provides the most intimate glimpses of work and first steps in cooperation. Interviews with several families supply some positive examples.

In a nuclear family with one or two children, relationships tend be close, intense, and focused. A positive effect is the extra time and attention that the child may receive.

When Erwin and his three-year-old son Mark, an only child, were busy repairing the garden fence, Dad said to his son. "Thank you, Mark, for helping me today."

"I'm not just helping you. I'm working," replied Mark.

A three year old already grasped the personal and social dimensions of work!

Interviews with two large families revealed practices common to both: organization, early training, and cooperation.

Danny and Angie reported how they managed a family with eight children. Danny, an experienced banker, decided that as parents they needed to initiate and apply organizational processes at home to bring order into family life and introduce their children to cooperative work.

Now ranging in age from seventeen to thirty-six, the children look back at their experiences and try to imitate their parental role models.

When the children were young, Danny already organized them into work teams; he posted their chores on the refrigerator, e.g., each team was assigned a specific night for dish washing. Danny and Angie trained the children in other age-appropriate tasks and followed up on implementation. Angie acknowledged that it was not always easy to observe the schedules; the children resisted, especially as they matured into adolescence and had less time for chores.

Danny also wanted to train his children in the art of handling money, so he established weekly allowances. If bigger special household tasks needed to be done, like cleaning the house screens, he offered extra money as an incentive. Once, when Angie was out of town and Danny wanted to invite guests for dinner, their children took over and established a division of labor. They undertook all of the preparations cooperatively and much to Angie's delight staged a successful dinner party.

Trixie, mother of eight, relates a special memory of an occasion when her children surprised her with their industry and enterprise. Her husband and she had to take an unexpected three-day trip out of town. Although in-laws were within reach to monitor the children, nevertheless, eldest daughters Inna, age eighteen, and Bessie, sixteen, were in charge. Trixie entrusted them with the responsibility of running the household in her absence. She prepared a cloth wall hanging with pockets to contain the daily allowances and lunch money that each child would need. Having prepared some of the meals for them, Trixie suggested simple foods for breakfast. She was apprehensive but confident the children would survive on their own.

Upon their return, both parents were amazed to see everything in place. The children had hung more hooks in the bathrooms to accommodate each child's towel. To streamline the flow of the daily routine, the children even suggested to Trixie some revisions in their usual schedule. Early training had clearly paid off. Family cooperation was the reward.

The School Setting

Transitioning from home to school, the child learns about cooperation on a grander scale. The school and teachers must unite in cultivating an environment where mutual respect, cooperation, courtesy, gratitude, and kindness are highly valued. Here are several suggestions.

- Establish a school culture that values team-building and cooperation.
- Tangibly promote the virtue of cooperation in the school: posters, school publications, memos, and contests that establish a school motto about cooperation; survey questionnaires that monitor current school morale and cooperative spirit are useful.
- Organize workshops, school assemblies, programs, and parenting seminars that advocate cooperation and school spirit.
- Schedule regular parent-teacher conferences and follow-up.
- Strengthen interpersonal relationships in the school community through workshops and programs to foster mutual respect and the sharing of good

practices among teaching and non-teaching staff in the various departments and at the various levels.

- Establish a 'buddy system' among students at the same grade level that will build positive and helpful relationships.
- Establish a 'big brother system' to encourage older students to help younger students.
- Organize a welcoming committee of students to orientate newcomers.

Respect for the dignity of others is the foundation of cooperation. Respect nurtures a multitude of other good habits: understanding, empathy, justice, and good citizenship that honor both the individual and the community.

Early Childhood: *Small Beginnings*

"Matt, it's time for dinner. Wash your hands first." So says every mother, probably every day.

"But Mommy, I want to play," protests Matt, probably every day.

This scenario plays out often and reflects the satisfaction children take in play. Matt's play is not a frivolous, aimless activity. Through exploration, he is interpreting the world around him and trying to find meaning and purpose in what he sees or experiences.

Play gives glimpses into the child's interpretations of situations and helps him/her find solutions. For example, through play in war-torn countries, children express their fears and reactions. When they find solutions through play, they will likely feel in better control of their experiences. By switching roles in play, they also get to see several perspectives of the players in the scenario.

Play satisfies a basic inner need to learn, i.e., to build, imagine, and solve problems. Imagine how the creativity of the child is challenged when he/she discovers how many ways six Lego bricks of the same color can combine—915,103,765![5] But there's a problem now. "Of all the factors affecting play today, few have a more worrisome impact than the recent changes in toys. The kinds of toys that are multipurpose and unstructured, like clay, blocks, generic toy figures, and baby dolls, encourage play that children can control and shape to meet their individual needs over time. Unfortunately, most of today's best-selling toys promote highly structured play. They're usually action figures or video games linked to TV programs or movies. They 'tell' children how to play and can channel them into merely using the toys to try to imitate what they see on TV or in the movies."[6]

Play is a source of development in all domains: physical, cognitive, emotional, moral, cultural, and social. Its relevance to social development is particularly strong because play nurtures a wide range of socialization skills: cooperation, communication, compromise, negotiation, friendship, respect, healthy competition, good manners, and patience. As social beings, children need to learn the art of cooperation as early as possible.

Early nurturance prepares the child to do good work. Through play in early childhood, children engage in dramatic play (the ability to pretend and imagine) and constructive play (the ability to build things and cooperate with others).

As social beings, children need to learn the art of cooperation as early as possible. The ability to cooperate prepares the child for future work that can spell the difference between work that promotes excellence and solidarity and work that undermines quality and harmony.

Play is of such importance that Article 31 of the United Nations Convention on the Rights of Children states that children and young people below eighteen have the right to play. Parents, caregivers, and teachers are challenged to integrate work and play and sustain an effective balance.

Opportune Moments

To foster cooperation in Early Childhood (3–6 years)

- Treat each child with respect and good manners and require the child to respond with 'please,' 'thank you,' and 'sorry.' This promotes respect for the dignity of another and facilitates positive interaction.

- Role play situations in class that demonstrate when, why, and how to thank one another or ask for permission or express regrets.
- Train the child in good listening habits; play the 'silence game' so that the child learns how to hear and understand directions and explanations. This ability contributes to the functioning of a cooperative group activity, whether at home or school.
- Train the child how to take his/her turn in a family or group activity. This promotes mutual respect, good manners, and cooperation.
- Assign regular household chores (tidying up toys, setting the table, putting laundry back into drawers). Emphasize that each family member contributes to the functioning of the whole family.
- Review the goals of a family activity, such as taking a family trip. This motivates children to fulfill their respective tasks and keeps the activity and family togetherness on track.
- Encourage the child to share his/her ideas that will foster cooperation in a group activity. Ask him/her, "How can we work together in a better way?"
- Guide siblings in sharing toys. Set a time limit for each child to play; keep the other child occupied with another activity. Eventually, this practice turns into a routine and children learn that they cannot monopolize a possession or always get their way.
- Encourage children to share their discoveries and experiences. This generates a collective spirit of awe in learning.
- Play with children to demonstrate give-and-take cooperation; avoid imposing or dominating the activity.
- Gradually introduce children to sports and games.
- Explain the concepts of winning and losing in simple terms with examples and stories. Younger children are not cognitively mature enough to grasp the concepts and react emotionally. It is best *not* to focus on scores and winning.
- Emphasize the importance of playing fair so as to minimize competition at this stage. Help the child understand that he/she will not always win in a game.

- Emphasize that in a sport or game he/she must show good manners, control him/herself, and not harm another player.
- In school, plan activities that allow children to work together with a partner or buddy, e.g., children share a book and alternate turning the pages; children paint a mural together (each child could be responsible for a certain section or color); or children garden and cultivate a flower patch.
- Plan developmentally appropriate games requiring teamwork, for instance, provide building blocks in the classroom and group children together to construct something related to the class lesson.
- Engage pupils in a school-wide cooperative endeavor, such as picking up litter. Have children wear protective gloves during the activity.
- Let a child explain the class routine and rules to a new student.
- Encourage a child to assist the teacher in distributing or collecting papers; rotate the duty.
- Encourage a child to help a classmate who is having difficulty with a task or activity.
- Suggest that children could share their snacks with a classmate who does not have any.
- Read stories about working together and the joy that cooperation brings.
- ROLE MODEL COOPERATION.

A Problem in the Process: Poor Attachment Bond

An attachment bond with a consistent caregiver is the foundation of a child's ability to cooperate. This bond forms in the earliest years of life, between six months and two years. When the child receives sensitive and responsive care, he/she feels secure and protected and (1) is more likely to develop a positive self-image and the healthy self-respect of one who feels he/she is worthy of love and care; (2) is inspired to develop trust, empathy, and caring for others; and (3) learns first lessons in cooperation.

Under ordinary circumstances, parents, as the primary educators of the child, play crucial roles in the attachment process and in building future relationships. Others who may contribute significantly to the child's formation of a consistent, emotional bond include grandparents, siblings, other family members, nannies, teachers, and neighbors.

Parents promote attachment by sending the child verbal and nonverbal messages and signals that he/she is lovable. Quite naturally, the child responds and a loving connection is formed. Especially in times of illness, injury, and stress, the child likely prefers the attachment figure. This dynamic give-and-take process reflects an enduring, reciprocal emotional tie in the making. It paves the way for cooperation in activities directed to mutual benefit.

Research identifies several patterns of attachment: secure, avoidant, ambivalent, and disorganized.[7] A secure attachment is the forerunner to the formation of cooperation. Two examples illustrate the process.

With years of teaching experience, Pamela is on the right track as she trains her son Connor in socialization skills. Her studies in education and childhood development have served her well as she reinforces the art and craft of cooperation.

Connor was a lovable, easy-going baby by temperament, so attachment was natural for him, his parents, and grandparents. He responded well to Pam's affection, chatting, reading, laughing, and bonding as they took walks, spent time on the beach, visited friends, and played with toys. Because Pam and her husband John provided for his needs with consistency and caring, a secure base was formed. They noticed that Connor hardly ever manifested anxiety regarding strangers and even initiated conversations with visitors. He was not afraid to go beyond his secure base and explore his surroundings.

As a firstborn, Connor needed a wider base for socialization, so Pam invited over neighborhood children to play. She arranged for play dates, visited grandparents, and enrolled him in preschool and other community programs. An outgoing child, Connor's confidence and friendliness blossomed. Well-mannered and eager to play and cooperate with other children, he has all the makings of a future mayor!

Even as a busy corporate executive, Kathy has developed a secure attachment with her daughter Lynette by devoting herself to the child on evenings and weekends. Sebastian is a hands-on father and very supportive husband. But Kathy still feels twinges of guilt each day when she leaves for work, and Lynette, now three, has a separation anxiety; the child cries and clings to her mom. Fortunately the nanny, Josephine, has bonded well with Lynette, so the child is adjusting to the leave-taking. Her entrance into preschool will soon expand her world of play and friends.

Kathy and Sebastian have wisely learned how to ease the separation anxiety through several parenting techniques. (1) Both parents talk about their work in an upbeat manner to help Lynette view work as a satisfying activity. (2) Both have brought their daughter to their workplaces. (3) By giving simple explanations, they tell the child what they do and why they work. (4) Kathy has established a daily routine to signal that the time for her departure is approaching: mother and daughter sing the song, "So long, farewell, Auf Wiedersehn, Adieu" from *The Sound of Music*. It actually works! (5) Mom and Dad make spot-checks and telephone Lynette from the office. (6) Kathy gives her daughter a 'transitional object' (her perfumed handkerchief) which the child puts in her pocket to reassure and remind her of Mom's return. (7) The parents and Lynette plan in advance what bedtime story they will read at bedtime.

All of these planned activities have comforted and responded to Lynette's need for reassurance. Her reactions to her parents' departures are actually indicators of a securely attached child who looks forward to their return. These meaningful techniques and gestures of love develop in the child the capacity to give love and show empathy to others.

Middle Childhood: *Room for Improvement*

Middle childhood is the 'play age.' At this stage, children are capable of engaging in formal play that requires an understanding of rules and penalties. They are better able to control emotions, socialize, and deal with competitive situations. Because of their developing maturity, they can go beyond the 'me' level to the 'we' level and cooperate with others.

Children raised by parents who are either permissive or authoritarian experience an ineffective exercise of authority that could undermine their ability to cooperate.

The spoiled, pampered, and overprotected child may become selfish, insecure, lack self-discipline, assert a sense of entitlement, or face exclusion from a group. Instead of internalizing empathy, helpfulness, and a spirit of service and cooperation, he/she may manipulate others and set him/herself up for loneliness.

On the other hand, the child who has been raised by authoritarian, harsh, threatening parents will incline toward defiance, rebellion, aggression, and retaliation, or the other extreme—timidity, insecurity, indecision, and lack of self-confidence. The autocratic approach to discipline is likely to lead to difficulties in the child's socialization and failure to develop the virtue of cooperation.

Opportune Moments

To foster cooperation in Middle Childhood (7–12 years)

- Envision the family as a team with different roles and duties assigned to each member. Duties can be posted and periodically changed to foster better teamwork.
- If the family is having a party, involve children in the tasks. They can set the table, serve food, hang up coats, and plan games.
- Let the child hand gifts to the one being celebrated; this fosters kindness and allows the giver to see the joy of the recipient.

- Involve the child in the upkeep of the home; this motivates family solidarity.
- Involve the child in menu planning, cooking, and baking in preparation for future independence.
- Train the child in good study habits and encourage him/her to help siblings and classmates internalize self-discipline in studies.
- Suggest that the child donate toys or books to the less privileged.
- Guide the child to befriend like-minded peers who share interests and a common value system. Welcome the child's friends for a play date to get to know them.
- Encourage the child to befriend or help the underdog, e.g., in bullying situations.
- Suggest that the child join school clubs, but be cautious not to overschedule the number of activities.
- Communicate effectively with the child by listening first. Be a friend without diminishing parental authority.
- Organize a family council to discuss plans, establish family routines, or solve family conflicts.
- Encourage the child to share happiness and joyful experiences with family, friends, classmates, caregivers, and teachers.
- In the later years of middle childhood, encourage the child to join alternative projects that are service-oriented (neighborhood or outreach projects, storytelling to orphans, peer tutoring, apprenticeship programs).
- Motivate the child to pursue a sport that is of interest and requires teamwork.
- Suggest that in team sports the child should shake the opponent's hand before and after the game, win or lose.
- At school, organize a group research project (or ask students to initiate one about an issue that interests them). Let the students assign each member an individual role. When the research project is completed, let the group present the results of their study.

- To encourage creativity, students can design the materials needed for a project. To meet deadlines, guide children to work cooperatively.
- Train the children to devise rules and sanctions that govern the project; then let them implement them and take the consequences.
- Make it clear to students that each member's participation is vital to the completion of the project.
- If possible, students can perform their project in another class to share their accomplishments, e.g., a puppet show version of their project.
- ROLE MODEL COOPERATION.

A Problem in the Process: Cyber-bullying

Bullying occurs when one or more stronger, more powerful children repeatedly prey upon, frighten, or deliberately hurt a weaker child who cannot stop the aggression and defend him/herself. The abuse can be physical, verbal, or relational. (This latter includes humiliating, ostracizing, or not including a child in a group.) Clearly, cooperation is not part of a bully-victim relationship.

Although bullying has always been a common family headache in situations of sibling rivalry, school-based bullying has the potential of becoming a 24/7 ordeal because children extend the bullying via cyberspace. With an upsurge of bullying-related suicides in puberty, parents and educators need to pay special attention to the behavioral indicators of the bully as well as the victim. Heretofore overlooked is a third party, the bystander who knows of or watches the bullying and is likewise affected. The bystander faces a choice of helping the bullied, standing up to the bully, or remaining on the sidelines.[8] He/she faces consequences for whatever choice is made.

In recent years, social media have emerged as powerful tools for socialization, cooperation, and helpfulness. Social media focus on a site or social network service that allows users to share ideas, activities, events, photos, and interests. Basically, social networking is web-based and provides means for users to interact over the Internet by such means as e-mail, instant messaging, and chat rooms. Popular methods now combine many of these, namely, Facebook, Twitter, and YouTube.

Several media-related problems in middle childhood interfere with the development of work habits and the virtue of cooperation. Through negative social networking, the child may (1) try to gain in popularity and acceptance by sending inappropriate messages and photos or (2) put down others through cyber-bullying, which has the potential of seriously undermining social relationships and distracting both the bully and the victim from their work.

At a recent parenting seminar, I listened to the alarm and disappointment of parents who learned of a stalker who was sending nasty, obscene messages to their twelve-year-old daughters. The stalker asked intimate, degrading questions. If the victim did not respond, the stalker retaliated by sending even nastier messages about the victim to a much wider number of subscribers. Parents were dismayed by the cruelty and lack of respect for the dignity of others. On the other hand, sometimes parents are painfully unaware of "parenting practices that foster bullying: a lack of warmth and involvement; permissive attitudes towards a child's abusive behavior, and reliance on physical punishment."[9]

As preventive measures, parents can exercise control over cyber-bullying. The following suggestions are adapted from Michele Borba's 'Six P's of Internet Safety.'

- Parental Presence: Announce upfront that the child's online activity will be monitored by the parent; the child should inform all his/her friends of this parental intervention.
- Public: Keep the computer in a public place in the home so that the child's use can be randomly monitored. Establish rules governing Internet use.
- Posts: Warn the child that there are no "take-backs" of messages; the latter become known to all recipients. Before messages are sent, the child needs to think seriously and prudently about whether he/she is about to send a message that could be harmful to another. If it will harm others, it must not be sent.
- Privacy: Insist that the child not share personal information, e.g., real name, address, phone number, passwords with people he/she meets online.

- People: Instruct the child never to go alone to meet a new 'friend' who has been met online. Rather, the child should be accompanied by a mature, responsible, and trusted chaperone. Parental permission should be given for a meeting.

- Please tell: Reassure the child that he/she should tell the parent if he/she feels uncomfortable, anxious, threatened, or senses that something is wrong in an online communication.[10]

It is reassuring to parents that they have the right and duty to exercise parental media management. By implementing control mechanisms, they foster cooperation between parent and child and act in the best interests of the child. Parental controls pave the way for the exercise of Internet safety.

Adolescence: *Best Efforts*

By adolescence, virtues are a work in progress and reflect training that has begun in childhood and finds further expression in adult life. Rae offers an example that illustrates how her husband Bill trained their sons in the habit of cooperation and spirit of service. "One year, we had a very snowy winter. I realized that there was more snow on the ground than many of the neighbors could safely shovel. Bill got the boys up and sent them to elderly neighbors. The boys willingly shoveled the sidewalks to prevent accidents. My daughter-in-law tells me that her husband, our son Danny, shovels the whole block, chatting all the way with the neighbors. And our son Michael travels thirty minutes from his house to shovel for me, without my ever asking him to do so. Children live what they learn!"

Opportune Moments

To foster cooperation in Adolescence (13–19 years)

- Alternate chores among siblings, assigning age-appropriate tasks. Follow up chores with reminders. Train the teenagers to demonstrate to younger siblings how to do the chores.

- Siblings could be assigned to work cooperatively in teams, with the older sibling in charge. The older sibling could escort the younger sibling to the school bus stop; guide homework assignments; or help care for a sibling who has a disability.

- Encourage the adolescent to visit and assist grandparents who live nearby.

- Encourage the teenager to volunteer in homes for the aged or foster care centers by reading to the residents, playing games, providing musical entertainment.

- Encourage the teenager to volunteer in neighborhood or school tutoring programs; join community projects that raise funds and foster awareness of worthy causes; or start a drive for newspaper recycling.

- Encourage participation in extracurricular activities that require active participation and helpfulness.

- Remind the adolescent (1) not to insist on his/her ideas and opinions in group projects and thereby jeopardize attainment of goals; (2) value the input of others; and (3) praise and encourage others in a group project.

- Under the teacher's vigilance and guidance, projects should be structured and executed in such a way that all project members have a role. In this way not just one or a few students end up having to do all the work.

- Teachers can assign group projects that require students to practice organizing a division of labor.

- Teachers should guide students in doing peer evaluation, especially if they have worked on a group project. This exercise can foster cooperation, objectivity, and fairness.

- Friendly competitions between teams in class teach students cooperation toward a common goal. Each student on a team must interact with and help the others in working for the best possible results as a team.

- Avoid excessive competition at home or in the classroom; this will prevent or minimize intense rivalry that undermines cooperation.

- ROLE MODEL COOPERATION.

A Problem in the Process: Peer Pressure

Adolescents' eagerness to belong makes them especially vulnerable to a multitude of influences. Peer pressure is one of the most powerful of these influences.

Peer pressure is a constraining force exerted on the teenager by a friend, classmate, peer group, clique, or gang that compels him or her to conform, accept, or imitate the thoughts, attitudes, and practices of another individual or group. Conformity generally means imitation of dress, grooming, language, manner of speech, or music preferences. It can include pressure in the choice of friends or participation in activities, such as going to parties or school dances. On a deeper level, peer pressure can be exerted to accept or not accept a value system, ideology, or code of behavior that supports or runs counter to work-related values and the practice of cooperation.

A teenager's ability to handle peer pressure is conditioned by internal and external factors, both positive and negative. Positive internalized factors include healthy self-worth, competence, self-confidence, clear-cut goals, and moral and spiritual values; negative factors include insecurities, low self-esteem, and lack of self-respect that undermine the teenager's ability to assert rights, opinions, and values. External factors that support the child's ability to withstand negative pressure include effective, authoritative child-rearing practices, family values and solidarity, good role models, and positive cultural practices; negative external forces include anti-values, blatant materialism, and the lures of consumerism.

Although peer pressure may be associated with risky behavior in adolescence (drug/alcohol abuse or delinquency), research indicates that "attachment to peers in early adolescence is not likely to forecast real trouble unless the attachment is so strong that the young person is willing to give up obeying household rules, doing schoolwork, and developing his or her own talents in order to win peer approval and popularity."[11]

Parental discipline plays a major role in counteracting negative peer pressure. "Authoritative child rearing is related to resistance to peer pressure. Teenagers whose parents are supportive and exert appropriate oversight respect their parents, an attitude that acts as an antidote to unfavorable peer pressure" (Maste 2001; Sim 2000). In contrast, adolescents who experience extremes of parental behavior—either too much or too little control—tend to be highly peer-oriented (Mason et al. 1996; Pettit et al. 1999). They more often rely on friends for advice about personal matters and their future and are more willing to break their parents' rules, ignore their schoolwork, use drugs, commit delinquent acts, and hide their talents to be popular with peers.[12]

Peer pressure can also take a positive direction; it may inspire imitation of admirable role models, motivate healthy change, and generate cooperation. Here is an example of positive peer pressure that inspires and restores confidence in today's youth.

Martin proudly tells of an incident involving his son Blake, age seventeen, a member of the school soccer team. The team played and won a championship match away from their home turf. In the aftermath of their victory, Blake's teammates wanted to celebrate by watching pornographic movies and drinking. Blake resisted the peer pressure of his teammates and convinced them to watch a newly released movie nominated for an Oscar. Afterwards, instead of drinking, they ate at a sushi bar and discussed the movie's messages of cooperation and courage. The team, inspired by the film, decided to organize an outreach sports program to help underprivileged children in a depressed area.

Blake's positive peer pressure set the stage for a team effort that brought great joy and hope to underprivileged children. His leadership was grounded in his integrity, self-control, responsibility, and ability to motivate cooperation.

Quotables: *Cooperation*

1. "Coming together is a beginning, keeping together is progress, and working together is success."[13]
2. "Great discoveries and improvements invariably involve the co-operation of many minds."[14]
3. "Honor bespeaks worth. Confidence begets trust. Service brings satisfaction. Cooperation proves the quality of leadership."[15]
4. My thoughts:

CHAPTER 5

PANCAKE DAY: *Cheerfulness in Work*

Spreading Joy

Word spread like wildfire when Mrs. Joos invited the neighborhood children for an afternoon snack. Delicious eight-inch German pancakes, crepe-like and paper-thin, could be filled with a choice of sugar, jam, applesauce, or fruit compote.

Even with four frying pans going on the stove at the same time, Mama could hardly keep pace with the demand for more of her delectable treat. The children knew that Mrs. Joos was exposing them to gourmet-quality cuisine and appreciated that she included them. She was a lovable, kind, cheerful neighbor!

In between mouthfuls, conversations were animated and ranged anywhere from sports to toys, story books, or the latest Howdy Doody television show. Life was simple and delicious in suburban New Jersey on a breezy spring Saturday.

As the years passed and children matured into adolescents, an eat-the-most-pancake-contest evolved quite naturally. It was not a contest to see how fast the children could eat the pancakes. Mama would never have allowed that. Instead, it was simply about who would eat the most and savor the taste until the next invitation came!

Mama's gesture satisfied the appetites of growing children. Through her culinary treasures and example of work values, Mama fostered solidarity and lifelong friendships in the neighborhood.

We sisters took great pride in watching how our Mama brought so much joy to our neighborhood friends, even if she assigned us to the clean-up committee!

....

As hard as Loretta and I have tried, we sisters have never been able to duplicate Mama's pancakes. She once explained her secret to us, but we just don't have her touch. Somehow her pancakes reflected Mama's lightness and goodness of spirit. The neighborhood children, now mostly grandparents, still remember the joy that Mama spread through her work and good cheer. "There is more joy in giving than in receiving," Mama often reminded us.

Cheerfulness is cultivated deep within. Even during trials and crises, Mama remained steadfast in her ability to exude a joyful soul. "God has a reason for everything! He is trying to teach us something."

Cheerfulness Defined

Characterized by an abundance of good spirit and ungrudging giving, cheerfulness is a virtue that shouts encouragement and gladness. It reflects simplicity and goodness of intention. A cheerful giver enlivens and animates others; he/she dispels worry and looks for the positive.

Cheerfulness is an ability to comfort and generate happiness. It is a virtue rooted in hope and faith; its foundation rests in confidence in God, others, and self.

As an overflow of a deeper spirituality and long-term struggle, the virtue rewards with a profound understanding of the meaning and purpose of life, love, relationships, and work. Sincere, chronic cheerfulness does not automatically come with age. It requires a daily struggle to trust in Goodness itself.

- Hand-in-hand with cheerfulness is the practice of:
- *Faith* or confidence, conviction, and trust in God
- *Optimism* or hope for the best; a look at the bright side of things
- *Patience* or uncomplaining endurance

- *Courage* or confrontation of difficulties and danger with firmness and without fear
- *Understanding* or discovery of meaning in experiences
- *Temperance* or self-control and self-regulation

True cheerfulness is characterized by a dynamic integration of these virtues.

"Hard Work, Simplicity, and Trust"

An interview about cheerfulness with a great-grandmother was bound to yield profound insights that could only come from reflection and wisdom. Linda, a charming, mentally sharp, and articulate ninety-one year old gladly shared her insights. We tried to focus our conversation, but it took many directions before we finally pinpointed three major components that accounted for Linda's cheerfulness and optimism: hard work, simplicity, and trust.

"Work makes us alive. If we don't have work, we worry, get bored, are idle, and may get sick. How can we be cheerful?" Although she is now frail in body, Linda still tries to garden. Otherwise, she reads, perseveres in her letter writing to bring good cheer to others, or visits those in need.

Concerned about the prevalent highly materialistic environment that easily clouds values and judgments, she advocated simplicity in thoughts, expectations, and needs. Her conclusion: "Simplicity is a way to happiness. When money, social climbing, and the search for prestige and lifestyle complicate goals, how easy to lose the way! Deep-rooted cheerfulness and peace are not possible. We need to look around us and see the simplicity, beauty, and order in nature to realize that we have gotten complicated."

Linda continued with her insights. "Even when good intentions and work are not appreciated, we need to seek the positive meaning of experiences, count our blessings, find joy in little things, and trust in God. He has a plan."

The real secret behind Linda's cheerfulness surfaced: her trust was anchored in God! Her cheerfulness was rooted in a solid foundation.

Fast Forward

Do the thoughts and advice of a great-grandmother resonate with today's youth?

Do young parents and their children appreciate the meaning and universality of cheerfulness as distilled from nine decades of life's experiences? Present-day positive anecdotes provide affirmation and evidence of the power of good cheer and optimistic values in the home and school settings.

The Home Setting

"It's easy to practice cheerfulness when everything is going right, but what about a family that has a special-needs child or someone suffering from chronic pain, is mentally challenged, or emotionally maladjusted?" A concerned father, hoping for some effective advice, asked this question during a parenting seminar on "Joy in Family Life."

In the course of interviewing parents, I met several families who had a special child. Their circumstance differed, but the families managed with remarkable, upbeat attitudes and coping techniques that worked.

Amy related a poignant family experience of how her family practiced cheerfulness and hope as they sought treatment for their nine-year-old daughter Monica's medical condition.

"Our doctor in Manila advised us to seek help in the United States for a rare kind of soft tissue benign tumor in Monica's foot. After careful consideration, we decided to relocate to California to obtain treatment. Despite the difficulties of adjusting to a different culture, for seven years we managed to adapt to life abroad.

"In a span of five years, Monica had five surgeries on her foot to remove the tumor. It continued to grow even after being resected. She went through several treatments, mostly experimental, because there is still no known cure for this kind of tumor. All treatments were short lived and held little promise.

"Just when we were on the verge of agreeing to amputation, another doctor suggested more surgery to remove the bulk of the tumor; the surgery seemed to work. Finally, at age thirteen, Monica was able to walk comfortably without limping. She went on with life and joined the high school dance drill team and became one of the lead dancers. She gave her best, knowing that the tumor could grow back and she would have to stop dancing. We resorted to natural medicine under the guidance of a biokinesiologist and the tumor has been stable for the past three years.

"We faced ups and downs during those years. Monica missed five months of school in seventh grade due to the bad side effects of the drugs; she suffered severe headaches and stomach pains. With the support of the school district, a teacher came to our home and tutored her when she was not in pain. When she finally attended the last three months of classes, she managed to get good grades.

"Monica thrived on the emotional support she received. Older sister Therese was always a big source of comfort. Among her simple gestures, she lent a favorite piggy stuffed toy when Monica was in pain. Our family of five children made sure that holidays were always a special source of togetherness, fun, and thanksgiving. We joined together to cook, bake, and play games. We encouraged Monica's friends to keep her company and to write letters after surgeries; they were always present during those times when she was lonely. For a three-month period, we traveled for a two-hour round trip to the medical center for Monica's weekly blood tests. Monica actually looked forward to the trip, because we would always go to her favorite noodle restaurant after the visit to the doctor. We were happy just being together and eating in a simple restaurant.

"Throughout the years, Monica persevered in doing household chores even if she had some difficulty walking. This gave her a sense of responsibility and confidence; it also kept her busy on weekends. When physically able, she attended summer camps and loved the activities and friendships she formed. She joined a Girl's Club and gave talks to the other members.

"Our experiences fostered family solidarity and Monica cherished the peaceful atmosphere which we tried to create for her at home.

I believe it was our natural acceptance of her condition without complaint that made her feel loved and supported.

"But it was spirituality that held us together. God's grace and Monica's faith truly explained her cheerfulness. Supported by the prayers of family, friends, and classmates, she never lost hope. During a time when she limped for six months, she only looked at the positive side of things even when her shoes were bulky because her tumor had grown big.

"Now that Monica's condition has improved and we are back in Manila, we remind ourselves how fortunate we have been to consult good doctors. Coping with any illness of a family member, especially a child, is a tough situation. It could have been a traumatic experience, but in our case it strengthened our trust in God. Cheerfulness comes from having a strong and unwavering prayer life which fortifies optimism, hope, faith, and unity."

With current interest and research focusing on autism, an interview with a parent gave glimpses into the concern, joy, and hope of raising an autistic child. Ann told about her happiness of welcoming a daughter who joined five brothers. "It was shortly after her first birthday when we noticed that Mara, a beautiful, lovable baby, suddenly did not respond anymore or turn to look when her name was called; she lost eye contact with people, and her speech did not progress. A developmental pediatrician suggested tests.

"At one and a half, Mara started therapy. By three, we received an official diagnosis of Pervasive Developmental Disorder Not Otherwise Specified (PDD-NOS), because Mara did not manifest all of the symptoms of autism. We did all we could to better understand her condition, attended seminars and conferences, read books, tried all kinds of diets and supplements, and enrollment in Auditory Integration Training (AIT) for autism. Now seven, Mara continues with therapies and special schooling.

"We know that in most cases, there really isn't any cure and that our Mara will have to deal with her disorder. As parents, we hope the symptoms will lessen and be kept under control so that

Mara lives a fairly normal, happy life. We have already seen signs of improvement. Mara now makes eye contact. What a blessing!

"Really, the most important step for us was acceptance. Early on, our sons managed that in a very natural way. They supported and stimulated responses in Mara and love her as she is. As a family, we could not allow ourselves to sulk or be devastated. Rather, we accept Mara as a child of God and have turned to therapies, faith, and prayer to care for this sweet, innocent, precious child who has brought us so much joy and whom we will always love."

The School Setting

Professional educators shed light on classroom practices that inspire cheerfulness in early childhood, middle childhood, and adolescence.

Gizelle, owner of a preschool, advocates starting the day with developmentally appropriate songs and sing-a-longs. Action songs are especially joyful for the young child. A happy environment is enhanced, especially if accompanied by physical exercise. Teacher Lexie advises creating a welcoming and encouraging atmosphere in which the child is not intimidated and knows that if he/she makes a mistake, there are solutions to problems. Teacher Ginny generates excitement and joy in learning by asking, "Guess what we're going to do now?"

With thirty-five years of teaching experience in middle school, Marietta makes sure that her classroom is a safe, fair, and good place to be. Drawing on a large reservoir of teaching strategies, she makes learning positive by including games and races. By telling her class "we are a family and need to treat each other with respect," she creates a caring environment that is happy.

With adolescents, teacher Carl assigns activities that are challenging and fun. He recognizes that in this age of media and technology, students are harder to motivate; therefore teachers need to know the students' interests. When students are interested and realize they will learn something, they find satisfaction in their assignments. Inspired, they find joy in learning and eventually take initiatives on their own.

Rae starts each day in her classroom with a big smile and an optimistic "Good Morning." Her cheerfulness is contagious. Another teacher, Concha, likewise suggests being conscious of one's disposition when entering the classroom. Children, especially teenagers, take the cue.

Based on their observations and experience, we see a familiar and natural progression: the young child thrives on a release of physical energy and enthusiasm in a positive, reassuring atmosphere. In the middle years, away from family for longer periods of time, the child is happy in an environment that is secure, fair, respectful, and filled with learning discoveries. By adolescence, the teenager finds joy and satisfaction when his/her interests and creativity are tapped.

Early Childhood: *Small Beginnings*

One of the greatest sources of happiness in life is the sight and sound of a baby laughing. The whole baby gets involved, with squeals of laughter accompanied by full-body movement. The baby's joy, although at times short lived and quickly followed by tears, is a universal emotion that points to cheerfulness in the making.

The witty and clever perceptions of young children indicate a developing sense of humor, goodness of intentions, and mischievousness. From our family treasure chest of witticisms come the following memories.

Our resident joker, Ricci, attended a birthday party where he had his first taste of Coca Cola at age three; he loved it. At home, beverages for the children were limited to milk, fresh juices, and water. Knowing I would not agree to his drinking Coke, at least not yet, he devised a clever plan to get his way.

"Mommy, may I have beer?" he requested.

"Beer? You cannot have beer. That's for grown-ups," I responded, rather amused by his request.

"But I want a glass of beer just like Papa," he insisted.

"No, that's not possible. Drinking beer is for adults. . . someday, when you're older."

"Okay. May I have a glass of Coke?" he asked with an impish smile.

When dad Enrique was hospitalized with burns resulting from an accident, we joked with three-year-old Ricci and asked, "Dr. Ricci, what do you prescribe for your patient to help him recover?" He answered with the precision and expertise of a specialist. "Bring me my hammer and some *aspilets*." He did not pursue a medical career!

When Anton, age two, playfully boxed with me, big brother Ricci at six reacted with the wisdom of an older brother. "Anton, don't box Mommy! Don't you know she's an antique?"

By age six, our resident philosopher Anton gave me wise advice.

"Mommy, you know how you can live to be one hundred? Eat a good diet. Work hard. And pray to God."

In amazement, I asked, "How do you know all of these things?"

"You have to find them out for yourself. Or sometimes I make things up and I find out they're really true! My brain gives me the answers."

Shortly afterwards, Anton came to another major conclusion about his own stage of development.

"Mommy, I like being a little boy. Childhood really grows me up!"

Indeed, he got it right. Childhood only comes around once in a lifetime. It should be a stage in the lifespan when wit, cleverness, and joy abound and the child becomes predisposed to an optimistic perspective on life, love, and work.

Opportune Moments

To foster cheerfulness in Early Childhood (3–6 years)

- Let the child do things for him/herself and experience the joy and satisfaction that comes from doing a task or finishing a chore.
- Explain that tasks well done bring happiness and satisfaction. These are the real rewards of work.
- Show appreciation for the young child's work. This will encourage the child to persevere and bring him confidence and hope.

- Show excitement and optimism about learning new things. This animates the child to take initiatives and find joy in discovery.
- To inspire cheerfulness and happiness in others, encourage the child to make creative cards to give to family, friends, classmates, patients in hospitals, or residents in nursing homes. This will help the child become a cheerful giver.
- Young children are remarkably empathic. Encourage them to show their understanding of others.
- Train the child to greet and thank elders. This gesture of good manners generates happiness and respect for others.
- Begin early literacy to motivate the joy of reading.
- Plan get-togethers and excursions that promote family solidarity, good cheer, a sense of security, and an appreciation of family history.
- Young children are especially sensitive to adult facial expressions. Show them generous smiles.
- The optimism of parents, caregiver, and teacher is contagious. Children are great imitators.
- Avoid physical punishment that does not respect the dignity of the child. Rather, give simple, clear, and firm explanations and reasonable, appropriate sanctions. Provide structure, set limits, and establish parameters for behavior.
- Encouragement brings joy while harsh discipline and put-downs lead to discouragement.
- At school, if a child looks sad or is frustrated, distract the child with a satisfying activity. Try to point the problem in a positive direction. If a pattern of depressive behavior continues, consult a qualified psychologist.
- Give the child reasonable flexibility and movement at home or in the classroom. This provides an outlet for the exuberance of young children.
- Provide indoor and outdoor play activities to channel the child's energies positively.
- ROLE MODEL CHEERFULNESS.

A Problem in the Process: A Challenging Temperament

Jermaine, Frankie, Lizette, Marlies, Animesh, and Harry, classmates in the same daycare center, were invited to Lizette's third birthday party. It was held at a recreation center boasting the latest gymnastic equipment, playground furniture, trampoline, plastic balloons into which the children could jump, and plenty of space to run.

Trained assistants and eager parents supervised the children, who were given free reign. The setting was perfect to glimpse differing temperaments that had already emerged at this young stage.

Upon arrival, Jermaine and Frankie adapted immediately and jumped into the balloons, cheerful, relaxed, and outgoing. Shy, sensitive, and cautious at first, Marlies and Animesh paused at the entrance to get their bearings. Clinging to a parent, they observed the tumultuous scene, but in time joined in the fun and had a ball. Harry, impulsive, high strung, and forceful, disrupted some children who were patiently waiting to jump on the trampoline. Lizette, the birthday celebrant, took things in stride and was very approachable as she stood center stage on her special day.

Their teacher, Gail, commented that the children's behavior was consistent with their conduct in the classroom. We were getting first-hand glimpses of the interplay of *nature* (temperament) and *nurture* (child rearing).

Temperament is a style of behavior that is partially inherited and already observable in the early months of life. It is a physiological predisposition to react in a certain way to people, new situations, and changes. Early researchers classified temperament according to characteristic mood, energy, and reactivity levels; *easy* (adaptable and positive); *slow-to-warm-up* (shy and cautious); and *difficult* (negative and irregular).[1]

Later findings produced three other temperament classifications: positive approach, extroversion, and lack of inhibition; negative affectivity, with a tendency toward shyness and inhibition; and effortful emotional self-control and self-regulation.[2]

Five especially challenging types of children have received considerable attention: the highly sensitive, self-absorbed, defiant, inattentive, and active/aggressive.[3] These are the shy, withdrawn, hyperactive, and violent children whom parents, caregivers, and teachers may deal with at home or in the classroom.

Temperament plays an obvious role in influencing the children's developing potential for cheerfulness. Jermaine, Frankie, and Lizette are consistently easy-going, upbeat, willing to participate, and see the brighter side of their experiences. Animesh and Marlies are shy, skeptical at first, and find it more difficult to socialize easily. Harry gets frustrated, tends to throw tantrums, and is demanding. He affects the sense of joy in others.

Parents, caregivers, and teachers may encounter several temptations in dealing with difficult children. These include the inclination to label children and cast doubts on the difficult child's adaptability; concern that the difficult child is doomed to maladaptive behavior and unhappiness; and lack of trust in the child's potential to overcome and gain control of a challenging temperament.

A sound understanding of the dynamic interplay of *nature* and *nurture* will be helpful to caregivers. Following are several suggestions to parents, caregivers, and teachers who have shy children like Animesh and Marlies or more defiant children like Harry. (The recommendations apply to both temperamental dispositions.)

Help the child know him/herself, i.e., become self-aware of his or her own temperament:[4]

- When a conflict arises, guide the child towards problem-solving.
- Show empathy for the difficulties the child may have in trying to gain self-control. Encourage the child to keep trying.
- Break challenges into manageable steps.
- Establish trust and a sense of security.
- Negotiate limits, if necessary.

Nature and *nurture* both play roles in predisposing the child towards cheerfulness. Parents, caregivers, and teachers can best facilitate the process through clear, firm, consistent, reassuring guidance and a cheerful disposition. They need to guide the child to cope with the demands and constraints of difficult situations.

Middle Childhood: *Room for Improvement*

Often considered the calm before the storm of adolescence, middle childhood is a vital period during which children form attitudes towards themselves, their emotions, schooling, social relationships, the family, and the world around them. Logical thinking and a more discriminating thought process increase. While children of this age love goofy jokes and giggle and laugh a lot, they are in continuing need of reality checks, positive reinforcement, and challenges that prove to them that they can accomplish what they set out to do.

Opportune Moments

To foster cheerfulness in Middle Childhood (7–12 years)

- Continually demonstrate the art of smiling, especially in the face of a problem, setback, or suffering. This does not deny the problem; rather, it reflects a sense of control under stress and optimism that solutions are possible.
- Guide the child in problem-solving to gain control of him/herself. This develops confidence and the ability to seek remedies through hard work and patience. The child will learn lessons in responsibility and optimism and avoid discouragement and pessimism.
- Remind the child of the uselessness of complaints, especially about homework and chores; complaints reinforce a negative attitude and undermine cheerfulness.
- Demonstrate that a happy, positive person shows enthusiasm and lifts the morale of others. A sense of humor goes a long way.

- Try to discover the special or hidden talents of the child. This fosters self-confidence, self-identity, and joy.
- Chores can be fun! Enlist a sibling's help in cleaning up smudges and fingerprints on the walls. Not only do the children work in the process, but they laugh and bond as well.
- If the child makes an error, remind him/her that valuable lessons can be learned from mistakes; ask what he/she has learned. Guide the child to understand the greater purpose or reasons for setbacks, i.e., they can learn something positive and helpful for the future.
- By continuously enrolling in courses or attending seminars and workshops, parents convey a love of learning. This sets a good example.
- Considering the impact and distractions of media, the teacher needs to include creative and alternative techniques that provoke interest and joy in learning.
- ROLE MODEL CHEERFULNESS.

A Problem in the Process: Pessimism

By temperament, some children tend to a predominant mood of gloominess, characterized by worry, whininess, and emerging pessimism. A child prone to such melancholy is especially vulnerable to setbacks, disappointments, frustrations, or losses. When fears of failure, rejection, abandonment, and changes complicate the child's life, the exercise of cheerfulness is seriously compromised.

Julianne and Mitchell saw that their nine-year-old Jimmy had a tendency to complain about homework assignments. If asked to complete a chore, he made excuses and cited obstacles. When his classmates excluded him from a game, he whined about how unfair they were. Basically, Jimmy always saw the dark side. His parents commented that he was his own worst enemy.

Although well-meaning, some parents may undermine the optimism that immunizes the child against pessimism. Following is a chart that adapts and consolidates three parental mistakes that undermine optimism; negative messages sent to the child; and positive suggestions to counter pessimism.[5]

Parental Mistake	Negative Messages Sent to the Child	Positive Suggestions that Counter Pessimism
Denying reality; saying false things; not telling the child the truth about his or her weaknesses, inabilities, or mistakes	Reinforcement of the child's views of him/herself as a loser, because the child knows what is being said is not true	Validation of the child's accurate perception of his abilities and inabilities; explanations and problem-solving to help the child find his or her own solutions; encouragement of perseverance to develop capabilities
Doing things for the child; solving the child's problems	Affirmation of the child's helplessness; expectation that others should do things for him or her	Problem-solving with the child to help him or her find solutions, make choices, and take consequences
Not countering the child's bleak way of seeing things	Development of a pessimistic view of things and him/herself	Reinforcement of optimistic ways of looking at things to prevent giving up

Well-intentioned though parents are, they may unwittingly encourage an unrealistic self-perception and may discourage the child from working hard to improve and persevere. In contrast, effective parents, caregivers, and teachers are those who:

- guide the child to understand why things failed or didn't work out
- direct the child towards better choices and decision-making
- require the child to take responsibility for actions

- help the child to appreciate that through experience and hard work, he/she can take control of things, make necessary changes, and develop resiliency
- direct the child to avoid self-absorption, immediate gratification, and depression
- foster mastery of the virtue of optimism

When parents, caregivers, and teachers set an example of hard work reinforced by enthusiasm and optimism, the child becomes inspired to emulate the role model.

Adolescence: *Best Efforts*

Adolescents tend to equate happiness and cheerfulness essentially with fun, laughter, jokes, and carefree leisure. While these may generate momentary joy, genuine cheerfulness has more profound foundations. Adolescents are capable of seeking these foundations and viewing themselves objectively when given the proper guidance. When teenagers are led to face challenges and difficulties with optimism and hope rather than escape mechanisms, they find relief and satisfaction in knowing they can overcome obstacles and accomplish things.

Opportune Moments

To foster cheerfulness in Adolescence (13–19 years)

- Foster a congenial, respectful, humor-filled atmosphere that generates love and laughter, still the best antidotes to pessimism.
- Build up self-worth in the adolescent through guidance and encouragement instead of humiliation, belittling, name-calling, and shaming. Teenagers are especially sensitive to the injustice of verbal abuse but remarkably responsive to affirmation.
- Open doors to parent-adolescent communication by allowing the teen to explain the reasons why he/she feels your rules or restrictions are unfair or unrealistic.

- During these discussions, mutual respect for the dignity of the other must always be maintained. Beneficial compromises can be reached, because the teenager has been given an opportunity to speak his or her mind. In these discussions, clear, unbiased thinking and optimism are encouraged.

- Suggest that the teenager join outreach programs to tutor children. Organize trips to visit the sick, aged, orphans, and poor. These activities strengthen appreciation for personal blessings and bring good cheer to others.

- Explain to the teenager the difference between being sympathetic and empathic. Sympathy generates compassion and a sharing in grief, while empathy communicates understanding and support. Both bring joy to the giver and the receiver.

- Seek the teenager's participation in planning family excursions, trips, board games, and sports as positive, wholesome alternatives that counter exposure to the violence and pessimism he or she may view in videos, television, and films.

- Show appreciation for little things when the teenager shares his time and efforts with family, friends, classmates. Parental gratitude demonstrates good manners, a sense of justice, and confidence in the adolescent's ability to be helpful and hopeful.

- Role model a spiritual life grounded in prayer to show thanksgiving for blessings and the courage to overcome trials.

- A SMILE, even when having a bad day, demonstrates that something good can always be drawn from the day's events and experiences. A smile costs nothing and is contagious; it expels an atmosphere of doom and gloom and gives hope to the teenager.

- Talk about positive parental experiences at work. This is an effective way of transmitting work-related good attitudes and virtues.

- Be vigilant for the appearance of a brooding and pessimistic outlook in the teenager.

- Safeguard the teenager's mental health and well-being. Be sensitive to signs of depression (e.g., excessive sleeping, lack of interest, suicidal tendencies). Don't hesitate to seek competent professional help.

- Advise students not to exaggerate the difficulty of assignments or projects but to work with optimism and take one step at a time until the task is finished.
- Demonstrate the joy of continuous parental learning through seminars, reading, consultations, and courses. These activities affirm the importance of study as a continuing, lifelong activity.
- In the face of unemployment, parents need to set an example of optimism and self-confidence, along with self-discipline and prudence.
- ROLE MODEL CHEERFULNESS.

A Problem in the Process: Unhealthy Self-Worth

Several 'problems in the process' already encountered at previous stages undermine a child's ability to face obstacles with optimism and cheerfulness. They include a poor parental bond, learned helplessness, or pessimism. If not resolved, these problems may converge and intensify in adolescence.

Low self-esteem or unhealthy self-worth paralyzes an adolescent's ability to solve problems. Much analyzed, debated, and frequently misinterpreted, self-esteem is a product of self-perception. It is defined as the "self-evaluative part of the self-concept, the judgment children make about their overall worth. Self-esteem is based on children's growing cognitive ability to describe and define themselves."[6]

Research generally indicates that secure children who have healthy self-worth are more socially competent. The development of self-worth begins early and continues throughout life. It can be affected by changing circumstances and relationships. Many socializing factors influence the process: environmental (socio-economic level, cultural practices, and expectations), and relationships with key players in the child's life (parents, siblings, grandparents, nanny, teachers, friends, classmates).

Teacher Phil noticed that Stanley, age sixteen, was usually unwilling to start doing a task and persevere. Although he was a bright adolescent, something was holding him back. He made excuses and procrastinated, and seemed to lack confidence in his ability to do well. Discussions with the guidance department and other teachers indicated that Stanley was like this in all classes. Although cognitively very capable, he was sensitive to criticism and tended to underachieve.

Constantly compared with his gifted sister, Stanley felt he could never live up to parental expectations. He underestimated his own talents and thought of himself as a loser, incapable of any significant achievements. With spirits demoralized and his considerable potential untapped, Stanley settled for mediocrity. He felt that unless his accomplishments were as noteworthy as his sister's he might as well play safe and not even try. At the root of his attitude was a sense of self as incapable and unworthy.

What Stanley needed was guidance to help him express his feelings, evaluate his reactions, reassess his talents, understand the dynamics of family relationships, gain confidence, and develop healthy self-worth. In cases like this, professional intervention and spiritual guidance can supply important insights and inspiration to restore healthy self-respect.

If teenagers have parents, caregivers, and teachers who are responsive and demonstrate caring and encouragement, they will believe in themselves and feel empowered to trust in their own abilities. With renewed or restored confidence, teenagers will be convinced that hard work in studies, sports, or hobbies enable and ennoble future success. If they develop realistic, healthy self-evaluations that perceive strengths as well as weaknesses, they are better equipped to take risks and finish what they have started. They will adopt an optimistic outlook and be of good cheer, knowing that trust and confidence in God, others, and themselves are good choices to make.

QUOTABLES: *Cheerfulness*

1. 1. "When one door closes, another opens. But we often look so regretfully upon the closed door that we don't see the one that has opened for us."[7]

2. "The secret of joy in work is contained in one word—excellence. To know how to do something well is to enjoy it."[8]
3. "Work with cheerfulness, with peace, with presence of God. In this way you will also carry out your task with common sense. You will carry it through to the end. Though tiredness is beating you down, you will finish it off well; and your works will be pleasing to God."[9]
4. My thoughts:

POSTSCRIPT

Along the way, I found this book taking on a life of its own. Family, friends, colleagues, students, parenting seminar participants, and even strangers who wrote emails, played active roles by adding depth, cohesiveness, and practicality. Those who contributed helped tie up loose ends and give a final push to completion.

The Work of Children laid the foundations for this sequel by expounding on the meaning, purpose, and value of work. Several themes recurred in the first book:

- the nobility of human work
- the dynamic dimensions of work that embrace its purposes, e.g., economic, personal, social, cultural, and moral-spiritual
- the dignity of the worker, especially the child embarking on a process which requires considerable effort and struggle
- the inspiration and guidance of parents, caregivers, and teachers who motivate the internalization of positive work attitudes
- service to the common good rendered through good work
- love of God demonstrated through the pursuit of excellence in work

A natural follow-up that spawned *Good, Better, Best* was the need to specify work-related virtues and concretize the child's quest for good work.

At a recent conference on Character Education, Dr. Thomas Lickona reminded his audience of parents and teachers to view children as "adults-in-the-making," i.e., to see what they are now and to actualize their potentials through virtues. He explained that there are three components of virtue-building: (1) the *mind*—the child needs to know what he is doing; (2) the *heart*—the child must want to develop the virtue; and (3) the *hand*—the child needs to demonstrate the good habit in his or her behavior.[1]

Interviewee Leticia Sala, an experienced preschool and elementary school educator, cleverly integrated the practice of the five virtues highlighted in this book. "I find that playing with blocks is a wonderful activity for developing the habits of *diligence, order, responsibility, cooperation*, and *cheerfulness*. Stacking blocks higher and higher without toppling the structure promotes diligence; placing the blocks just right develops order; accomplishing the task brings joy; and putting the blocks away where they belong fosters order, helpfulness, cooperation, and responsibility. It is important to provide containers and organizers so that children realize that there is a place for everything. Children can also make play of picking up whatever does not belong on the floor, such as their toys, socks, books, pieces of paper. The wastebaskets that say 'Feed me' are catchy ways to promote awareness of their use. In the process, the children also learn accountability to the greater good of the class."

Parental, caregiver, and teacher respondents to the survey questionnaire suggested developmentally appropriate *Opportune Moments* to guide the child during several stages of development. *A Problem in the Process* further identified specific obstacles in the child's struggle to develop a virtue. For example, during early childhood, the child needs to regulate emotions, comply with instructions, do things for him/herself, develop a strong attachment bond, and get a challenging temperament under control.

Socializing in middle childhood in the expanded environment of school, the child faces potential distractions from exercising work-related virtues, e.g., bullying by classmates or parental over-scheduling of activities that leave less time for school work or simple, imaginative and creative play. From within, the child may suffer from pessimism, learned helplessness, or media-related addictions. These problems reduce the time for achieving goals and strengthening good work habits.

The adolescent may have to undo, re-do, or correct poorly formed attitudes like lack of motivation, poor work ethics, and unhealthy self-worth. External distractions like materialism and consumerism, media and technology, and peer pressure may compromise or undermine the teenager's struggle to exercise virtues.

As *Good, Better, Best* came together through research, interviews, focus group discussions, survey findings, course discussions, and parenting seminars, educating children in virtues emerged as one of the noblest ends of education. What better legacy can parents, caregivers, and teachers leave than the development of children's capacity for truth and goodness through work! "Let us realize that the privilege to work is a gift, the power to work is a blessing, that love of work is success."[2]

Although formation in work-related virtues can sometimes be a tiring, thankless, and overwhelming task, it is nonetheless an enormously rewarding activity because it is also a source of self-development. When we foster virtues in children, we strengthen our own virtues and are happy. "True virtue is not sad and disagreeable, but pleasantly joyful."[3]

Notes

Introduction

1. Esther Esteban, PhD, *The Work of Children: Helping Children Understand the Meaning, Purpose, and Value of Work* (New York: Scepter, 2009), p. 40.

Chapter 1 Good, Better, Best: Diligence in Work

1. Madeline Levine, PhD, *Teach Your Children Well: Parenting for Authentic Success* (New York: Harper, 2012), as quoted in L. Alphonse, "Are Parents Setting Kids Up for Failure by Pushing Too Hard for Success?" (www:yahoo.com.YahooShine/Team Mom).
2. Diane Papalia and Ruth Feldman, *Experience Human Development* 12th ed., (New York: McGraw-Hill, 2012), p. 197.
3. Daniel Goleman, *Emotional Intelligence: Why It Can Matter More than IQ* (New York: Bantam Books, 1995).
4. Eugenio Lopez III, Keynote Address, Pinoy Media Congress Year 6 (Manila: University of Santo Tomas, February 22, 2011).
5. "What is Addiction?" *Psychology Today*, www.psychologytoday.com/basics/addiction.
6. Brent Conrad, PhD, "Computer Game Addiction – Six Negative Effects to Avoid," http:EzineArticles.com?expert+Brent._Conrad_Ph.D.
7. Donna St. George, "8.5 Percent of U.S. Youths Addicted to Video Games, Study Finds," *Washington Post*, April 20, 2009.
8. St. George, *Washington Post*, April 20, 2009.
9. Papalia and Feldman, 360.
10. Martin Luther King, Jr, www.brainyquote.com/quotes/topics/topic_work.html.
11. St. Josemaría Escrivá, www.escrivaworks.org/book/the_way-chapter-39.html.
12. Frank Lloyd Wright, www.thinkexist.com/quotes/Frank_Lloyd_Wright/.

Chapter 2 Laundry Day: Order in Work

1. Maria Montessori, "Sensitive Period for Order,"www.dailymontessori.com/sensitive-periods/sensitive-period-for-order/.

2. Jane Brooks, *The Process of Parenting* 3rd ed., (Mountain View, Calif.: Mayfield, 1991), pp. 92–94.

3. Alvin Rosenfeld and Nicole Wise, *The Over-Scheduled Child: Avoid the Hyper-Parenting Trap* (New York: St. Martin's Griffin, 2001).

4. Paul Dux, Jason Ivanoff, Christopher Asplund, and Rene Marois, 2006 as quoted in Papalia and Feldman, p. 383.

5. Madeline Levine, www:yahoo.com.YahooShine/Team Mom.

6. www.wisdomcommons.org/virtue/94-orderliness/quotes.

7. Robert Southey, www.wisdomcommons.org/virtue/94-orderliness/quotes.

8. Thomas Alva Edison, www.brainyquote.com/quotes/quotes/t./thomased131294.html.

Chapter 3 A Working Mama: Responsibility in Work

1. Linda Eyre and Richard Eyre, *Teaching Children Responsibility* (New York: Ballantine, 1993).

2. Shirley Wang, "A Field Guide to the Middle-Class U.S. Family," *Wall Street Journal*, March 13, 2012.

3. Wang, *Wall Street Journal*, March 13, 2012.

4. Wang, *Wall Street Journal*, March 13, 2012.

5. Roque Carballo, "A Look into Man and His Values: The Six Core Moral Values" (Manila: Self-Empowerment-Foundational Program on Work Values, Institute for Ethics and Excellence in Enterprise, University of Asia and the Pacific, 1992), pp. 6–7.

6. Abigail van Buren, www.brainyquote.com/quotes/authors/a/abigail_van_buren.html.

7. Jim Rohn, www.brainyquote.com/quotes/authors/j/jim_rohn.html.

8. Josiah Charles Stamp, www.worldofquotes.com/author/Josiah+Charles+Stamp /1/index.html.

Chapter 4 A Summer Block Party: Cooperation in Work

1. Daniel Goleman, *Social Intelligence: The New Science of Human Relationships* (New York: Bantam Books, 2006).
2. Goleman, *Social Intelligence*, p. 4.
3. Papalia and Feldman, 411.
4. Papalia and Feldman, 411.
5. "Over 915 million ways to combine just 6 LEGO bricks," www.mernin.com/blog/2011/08/combining-6-lego-bricks/.
6. "Rethinking Children's Play," www.funfamilyeducation.com/outdoor-games/play/35262html.
7. Papalia and Feldman, 188–189.
8. Dolores Coloroso, *The Bully, the Bullied, and the Bystander* (New York: HarperCollins, 2004).
9. Michele Borba, PhD, "How Can Parents Prevent Bullying and Monitor Kids' Tech Activity?" as quoted in *Excellence & Ethics,* Center for the 4th and 5th Rs, SUNY, Cortland, School of Education, Winter/Spring 2012, p. 7.
10. Borba, p. 7.
11. Fuligni, Eccles, Barber, and Clements, 2001 as quoted in Papalia and Feldman, p. 410.
12. Laura Berk, *Infants, Children, and Adolescents* 5th ed., (Boston: Pearson, 2005), p. 613.
13. Henry Ford, www.brainyquote.com/quotes/quotes/h/henryford121997.html.
14. Alexander Graham Bell, www.inspirationalquotes4.u.com/alexanderbell/index.html.
15. James Cash Penney, www.brainyquote.com/quotes/authors/j/james_cash_penney.html.

Chapter 5 Pancake Day: Cheerfulness in Work

1. Alexander Thomas and Stella Chess, 1977 in Berk, pp. 258–259.
2. Mary Rothbart and John Bates, 1998 in John Santrock, *Life-Span Development* 9th ed., (New York: McGraw-Hill, 2004), p. 211.
3. Stanley Greenspan, *The Challenging Child: Understanding, Raising, and Enjoying the Five "Difficult" Types of Children* (Reading, Mass: Perseus Books, 1995).
4. Greenspan, *The Challenging Child.*
5. Martin Seligman, *The Optimistic Child* (New York: Houghton Mifflin, 1995), pp. 13–14.
6. Papalia and Feldman, 253.
7. Helen Keller, www.quotationsbook.com/authors/3972/Helen_Keller.
8. Pearl S.Buck, www.thinkexist.com/quotations/the_secret_of_joy_in_work_is_contained__in_one/218039.html.
9. St. Josemaría Escrivá, www.escrivaworks.org/book/the_forge-chapter-9.html.

Postscript

1. Thomas Lickona, PhD, Character Education Conference (Manila: Woodrose Paref School, AIM Conference Center, September 21–22, 2012).
2. David O. McKay, www.butifnot.com/authors/LSD/David_O_McKay.html.
3. St. Josemaría Escrivá, www.escrivaworks.org/book/the_way-chapter-31.html.

APPENDIX

Dear Parent, Caregiver, and Teacher,
I would like to invite you to participate in a survey of 'opportune moments' in the development of work-related virtues in children as they engage in work, e.g., play, homework, household chores, hobbies, sports. On the next page are descriptions of five work-related habits or virtues which I plan on including in my book. Descriptions for each virtue are given. Kindly give examples (in bullet points) of HOW you have developed these virtues in children in Early Childhood, Middle Childhood, and/or Adolescence based on your observations, experiences, and insights. You may also want to include anecdotes that would be of interest to the readers.

Thank you for your participation.

E. J. Esteban

STAGE OF DEVELOPMENT

	DILIGENCE	ORDER
Early Childhood (3–6 Years)		
Middle Childhood (7–11 Years)		
Adolescence (12–19 Years)		

DILIGENCE: *To persevere with patience • To pay attention to requirements of task • To produce quality work • To improve progressively • To bear difficulties and obstacles calmly and without complaint* **ORDER:** *To establish a plan, sequence • To understand purpose of work • To prepare and execute with precision, punctuality • To follow up* **RESPONSIBILITY:** *To approach work with a sense of duty and accountability to self and others • To take the consequences of actions and*

RESPONSIBILITY	COOPERATION	CHEERFULNESS

performance • *To take initiative for tasks and own actions* **COOPERATION:** *To work well on a team and attain goals in harmony with others* • *To develop sportsmanship in success as well as defeat* • *To grow in a sense of service and helpfulness to others* **CHEERFULNESS** *To approach work with optimism and willingness to learn and improve* • *To find happiness and satisfaction in tasks* • *To spread joy in the workplace and among others*

INDEX